The Educational Needs
of Minority Groups

THE PROFESSIONAL EDUCATION SERIES

The Educational Needs
of Minority Groups

by

ALFREDO CASTAÑEDA

RICHARD L. JAMES

WEBSTER ROBBINS

PROFESSIONAL EDUCATORS PUBLICATIONS, INC.
LINCOLN, NEBRASKA

Library of Congress Catalog Card No.: 74-83020

ISBN   0-88224-043-9

© Copyright 1974
by
Professional Educators Publications, Inc.

Contents

INTRODUCTION

The Minorities and the
American Dream

by

WALTER K. BEGGS

Dean Emeritus, Teachers College
University of Nebraska

James Truslow Adams, in his penetrating book, *The Epic of America,* points out that the unique gift to mankind of the American people is a "great dream." It is not a dream of material wealth or political power, it is not a dream of economic or industrial efficiency — although all of these things have been achieved or realized by the people of the United States. The American dream is unique because it holds the promise of "a land in which life should be better and richer and fuller for every man, with opportunity for each, according to his ability or achievement." Put another way, it is the dream of a "social order in which each man and each woman shall be able to attain to the fullest stature of which they are innately capable and be recognized by others for what they are, regardless of the fortuitous circumstances of birth or position."*

Many people find it difficult to see in the evolution of American society the great epic achievements described by Adams. The people of the United States, it is admitted, have had a different, and perhaps a unique, pattern of cultural experiences. They have been incredibly lucky, because they found a fantastically rich continent to exploit, and they were protected from foreign interference by two great oceans while they were exploiting it. Also, they were able to spread out over a vast frontier, which prevented crowding, and gave them a somewhat different set of values. Nonetheless, it is said, it is patently ridiculous to argue that these experiences, fortunate as they have been, have produced a radically different social and cultural format, or a fundamentally different social attitude, on the part of a whole nation of people.

As one examines the deficiencies, the ambiguities, the paradoxes — and, in some instances, the social injustices — that pervade modern American society, he is inclined to agree. And we could wonder, in our more depressed moments, whether our cherished dream is at best anything more than a mirage and at worst simply a vehicle for our hypocrisy when we speak of equality and justice, and freedom for all, and particularly when we use the expression "the American way of life."

*James Truslow Adams, *The Epic of America* (Boston: Little, Brown, 1931), p. 374. The phrase "The American Dream" may or may not be original with Adams. His book is, however, the earliest source where this author has noted it in print.

But the American epic and the American dream are worthy of a much more searching and deeper examination than this. It is certainly true that our society has not always developed in the direction envisioned by the dream, and that the people of this country have not always behaved in the way the dream indicates they should behave. Any skeptic, viewing this society, can point out and document hundreds of instances where individuals, or groups, or even whole sections of the populace have been denied equal opportunity, and in some instances forcibly restrained from enjoying their basic human rights. But to put the situation on balance, more people have achieved equality, and a larger section of the populace has had its rights protected, than anywhere else in the world. Historically it sometimes appears that a sort of sanctimonious bigotry must have possessed the "great" founding fathers of the nation, who were able to write nobility of intent into the Declaration of Independence, pronouncing all men free and equal, and a little later sanctioned human slavery in the basic law of the land—its Constitution. But again, on balance, that same Constitution was amended to abolish slavery, and subsequent amendments have attempted to protect and expand the rights of all of the people.

No, the American dream has not produced a Shangri-La or a model society, and maybe not even a very good society. The nation has never fulfilled its dream—or come close to fulfilling it. *But neither has the nation lost its dream*, or the capacity to dream it—or the will to attempt to achieve its promise. This is the significance of the mystique of the dream. It is not a formula which spells out in detail how its implications shall be achieved. It is not a set of criteria for measuring how well the society has performed in reaching its stated objectives. It is rather a constant, omnipresent challenge—an abstraction, the conscience of the people in composite, the producer of a guilt feeling, and hence a balance against prejudice and bigotry—and finally and above all, it is that mysterious quality in the American people which brings them back again and again, when the game appears to be lost, to do the things which need to be done to keep the promise of the "great society" alive.

And at the present time a great deal needs to be done. The nation faces grave problems and great challenges in many areas. In this presentation we shall confine our attention to some of the issues and problems that are troubling our system of education. We have always assumed that the schools of our nation are one of the great bastions of freedom and the entrée to most of the great things in American life. Unfortunately, we have also assumed that if the students in the schools were channeled through the same, or very nearly the same, curricular programs, somehow a sort of melting-pot effect would result, and the product of the schools would be readily assimilated into the mainstream of the culture.

In the past few years, however, some of the minority groups in American society have sharply challenged this thesis. It is maintained that the schools do not always, or completely, meet the needs of minority children — and, indeed, that in some instances they are indifferent, if not antagonistic, to their needs.

In this book it is our purpose to examine the needs of three of the great minority communities, the black Americans, the Mexican-Americans, and the Native American Indians. Each group has a distinct, if not a unique, history in its initial contact and subsequent relationship with the dominant strain of American culture. Each group has suffered traumatic experiences and some indignities, and even cruelty, at the hands of the majority. And each of these groups feels that the educational system has, in part at least, failed to meet its peculiar needs.

It is significant that in total numbers these three communities represent roughly 20 percent of the population of the United States. Practically all the members of these groups are full-fledged citizens of the nation, and their physical and social and economic well-being are vitally important factors in the general cultural health of the country.

We have asked three scholars, each with excellent academic credentials, each a bona fide member of one of the minority groups, to write an essay on the educational problems and needs of his group. Each of these men has demonstrated the ability to join and live comfortably in the dominant society. But each also has a complete knowledge and a deep understanding and respect for the cultural patterns of his own group.

We did not instruct or structure these authors in any way, except the general assignment for each to write about the educational needs of his group. The results follow in the next three sections.

The Educational Needs of Mexican-Americans

by

ALFREDO CASTAÑEDA

Professor of Education and Psychology
Stanford University

INTRODUCTION

The ethnic, racial, and social diversity characteristic of present-day American society makes it necessary to reexamine earlier philosophical assumptions concerning the role of education in dealing with minority groups. The present essay describes an alternative role. Understanding the educational needs of Mexican-Americans requires such a reexamination. Mexican-American cultural values and their role as determinants of teaching styles must be understood if we are to develop teaching and curriculum strategies more consistent with the backgrounds of Mexican-American children.

Several excellent publications delineating the educational plight of Mexican-Americans have recently appeared under the auspices of the United States Civil Rights Commission.[1] Also worthy of examination are a number of excellent publications covering a wide range of educational issues, problems, and suggested programs related to Mexican-Americans.[2] For readers interested in exploring the literary, political, historical, economic, and other aspects of the Mexican-American experience, an extensive annotated bibliography is provided at the end of this section.

CULTURAL DEMOCRACY AND AMERICAN PUBLIC EDUCATION

American public education has seriously jeopardized one of the three major features of American democracy. While American public education has continually attempted to keep alive the principles of political and economic democracy, it has been antagonistic to the principle of *cultural democracy*, the right of every American child to remain identified with his own ethnic, racial, or social group while at the same time exploring mainstream American cultural forms with regard to language, heritage, values, cognition, and motivation.

Many American children whose home and community socialization experiences differ from those of the Anglo-American middle class experience a school atmosphere, especially during the early years, which is forbiddingly alien. This atmosphere has had, historically, two essential themes; namely, strangeness and an explicit or implicit rejection of all socialization experiences that differ from it. The fundamental message to the child whose home and community socialization experiences are different has always been, Learn our ways and forget your own. Although this message has remained the same, the name for it has varied—for example, "melting pot," "assimilation," "Anglo-conformity," and so forth. An early example of this philosophy in the field of education is illustrated in the following remarks by Cubberly:

Everywhere these people settle in groups or settlements to set up their national manners, customs and observance. Our task is to break up these groups or settlements, to assimilate and amalgamate these people as a part of our American race, and to implant in their children, so far as can be done, the Anglo-Saxon conception of righteousness, law and order, and our popular government, and to awaken in them a reverence for our democratic institutions and for those things in our national life which we as a people hold to be of abiding worth.[3]

In a very straightforward way, this quotation establishes the "Anglo-assimilation" philosophy. The educator who agrees with Cubberly usually maintains that among all public agencies, the schools are most responsible for bringing minority children into conformity with mainstream American ideals. As a result, some educators have punished and humiliated children for doing things in the classroom that the children have been taught to do in their homes. Sincerely wishing to help their students and to prepare them for adult society (as they understand it), they have done whatever they felt was necessary to rid their pupils of "undesirable differences." Advocates of this philosophy do not feel that eliminating a child's cultural preference is undemocratic. Teachers have typically been so confident of their own values and goals that they have prevented children from choosing which part of their upbringing they would preserve and which part they would abandon or modify. Teachers have also overlooked the fact that a child's culture represents a real and solid world, a world daily demanding his loyalty, a world which has taught him how to think and feel and, most important, *how to learn.*

Cultural democracy is easily misunderstood. It should not be seen as a plea for separating or breaking up groups of people. Cultural democracy refers, rather, to the legal right of the individual to be different while at the same time a responsible member of the larger, dominant society. Cultural democracy refers to the idea that there are completely different, yet equally legitimate ways of choosing what one prefers to do and how and when to do it, and different ways of making judgments about what people do and think. Just as people of different persuasions on any subject interpret events differently, so do different cultures or ethnic groups prize different things. Different cultures or ethnic groups must live beside one another with respect and understanding for these differences. The best place for individuals to acquire this respect and understanding of others and themselves is in the school. Unfortunately, the public schools have not traditionally embodied the features of cultural democracy that would make this ideal a reality.

THE CULTURALLY UNDEMOCRATIC CHARACTER OF AMERICAN PUBLIC EDUCATION

It is possible to identify at least three distinct and major components of educational policy that are designed to implement the socialization function of education. These are (1) language and heritage, (2) cultural values, and (3) teaching styles. In the case of the first component, the goal is to facilitate the development of a healthy self-concept (identity) and one's role in and relationship to society. In the case of the second component, the goal is to facilitate understanding of society's standards of desirability and acceptance as well as the internalization of moral standards, or elements of conscience, which direct behavior along socially appropriate and productive routes. In the case of the third component, the goal is to render teaching styles appropriate to the modes of thinking, remembering, perceiving, and problem-solving desired by society.

If we examine the content of American public education in relation to each of these three components, it becomes eminently clear that what exists in our schools is a picture primarily descriptive of the language, heritage, values, and teaching styles characteristic of Anglo-American middle-class society. It is *monocultural*, or culturally exclusive, in conception, for the content of these three components does not reflect the language, heritage, values, and teaching styles characteristic of other cultural, racial, or social groups. Thus, American public education has failed, in each of these components, to provide the content that would enable minority children to develop healthy self-identities, to minimize cultural or value conflicts, or to learn by means of those preferred modes of cognition and motivation which are the result of their home and community socialization experiences.

THE NEED FOR DEMOCRATIC CULTURAL PLURALISM IN EDUCATION

Because American public education, operating under the melting-pot theory, has failed to provide culturally democratic educational environments, a new social philosophy must be formulated if the schools are ever to meet the educational needs of children who are products of socialization experiences different from those of the Anglo-American middle class. The basis for this reformulation is implied in the concept of cultural democracy, that is, the right of every American child to remain identified with his own home and community socialization experiences, regardless of whether these experiences are designated ethnic, racial, cultural, or social. This implies that the schools should actively contribute to the positive development and strengthening of these unique home and community socialization experiences *as valuable in their own right.* Furthermore, these culturally, racially, and socially unique home and community experiences should serve as the basis for exploring Anglo-American middle-class language, heritage, values, modes of cognition, and motivation. This is to suggest that a culturally democratic educational environment would incorporate into the educational process, with equal value, status, and importance, the language, heritage, values, and teaching styles of which any child is a product.

BICULTURALISM IN EDUCATION

Multicultural education (or *multiethnic education*) might be used as a term to designate the goals of exploring those aspects which are particularly characteristic of the racial, social, and cultural groups within which the child must learn to function competently and effectively. The process whereby this can be achieved for any child is more accurately termed *biculturalism.* That is to say, whatever these aspects are, the *basis* for exploration must be the language, heritage values, and cognitive and motivational modes of which the child is originally a product. This conception of democratic cultural pluralism in education implies that the educational goal of all children in American society would be that of learning to function competently and effectively in more than one cultural world, and of contributing to developments in more than one cultural world. This is in marked contrast to variants of the social theory of the melting pot, which set as its primary goal competent and effective functioning as well as contributions in only one cultural world, that of the Anglo-American middle class.

Differences in learning and incentive-motivational styles between members of different ethnic groups are the end result of socialization styles reflecting the values of ethnic groups. The middle points in this process are the teaching styles of the mothers and the resulting differences in the cognitive styles of the children. The entire sequence from values to modes of learning is shown in the diagram.

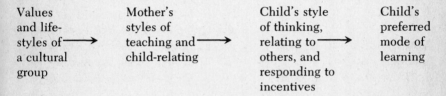

| Values and life-styles of a cultural group | → | Mother's styles of teaching and child-relating | → | Child's style of thinking, relating to others, and responding to incentives | → | Child's preferred mode of learning |

MEXICAN-AMERICAN VALUE CLUSTERS

Most Mexican-Americans reside in one of three basic types of community. These have been designated traditional, dualistic, and atraditional communities. The following description deals primarily with the values of the traditional communities, that is, those which are close to the Mexican border, rural in character, ethnically homogeneous (most residents are Mexican-American), and have strong historical attachments to Mexico. Elements of these same values, however, appear in the dualistic and atraditional communities but to a lesser degree. Thus, because of a variety of factors, there will be a diversity in the expression of these values. Several of these important factors will also be described.

Most Mexican-American values can be classified into one of four clusters: (1) identification with family, community, and ethnic group; (2) personalization of interpersonal relationships; (3) status and role definition in family and community; and (4) Mexican Catholic ideology.

Identification with Family, Community, and Ethnic Group

The traditional Mexican family and community structure develop in the individual a strong sense of identity with, and loyalty to, his family, community, and ethnic group. Since personal identity is so strongly linked with the family, a sense to achieve for the family is early developed in the child. This, it should be noted, contrasts with the more common definition of achievement—that is, for the benefit of the individual. This is consistent with recent findings, which indicate that in contrast to middle-class Anglo-American children, who often exhibit an achievement motive that mainly concerns the self, Mexican-American children appear to be motivated to make their families proud of them and benefit their families.[4] One immediate implication is that it is critically necessary that Mexican-American parents be involved in the educational process. Parental involvement strengthens the idea in the child that scholastic success is important to his family.

Achievement for the family appears to be generalized as cooperation achievement. To strive for individual gain is selfish. Individual competition is seen as destructive because it hurts family, community, and ethnic unity. Recent research indicates that Mexican-American children are more likely to adopt cooperative modes than Anglo-American children, even in the presence of adult cues that indicate competition.[5] These findings also help to explain why Mexican-American children are often described as not being "motivated" or "achievement oriented." Many suppress individual gain in favor of family, community, or peer group gain. Teachers could utilize this characteristic preference for a cooperative mode by assigning group projects which require children to work together.

This preference for the cooperative mode may also help explain the spirt of *La Raza* (the ethnic group), which centers on the belief that Mexican-Americans are united by a common spiritual bond and have a responsibility to help each other. One means of utilizing this idea would be the use of cross-age teaching. In this way, older Mexican-American children would be able to express their responsibility by helping to teach the younger students.

The ability and willingness to speak Spanish is also considered an important criterion of identity with the ethnic group. For this reason, encouraging Spanish fluency in Mexican-American children strengthens their self-concept.

Personalizing Interpersonal Relationships

Another set of values characterizing traditional Mexican-Americans is the humanistic orientation that results from the historical kinship and cooperative achievement aspects of relationships established in traditional Mexican communities. The implied commitment to help others leads to the development of sensitivity to the *needs* and *feelings* of other persons. This sensitivity is critical in both the nonverbal and the verbal realms of interpersonal relationships. It permits the individual to read and understand another person's feelings without forcing him to embarrass himself by pleading for help. This explains why Mexican-American children (especially males) seldom ask for help with their school work even though they may be doing poorly; they are accustomed to expressing needs in an indirect, nonverbal way that is often unfamiliar to many teachers, and in their own communities such indirect expressions always meet with a response.

In the traditional Mexican-American community, a person who has the capacity to help assumes the role of helper, knowing he can expect others, in turn, to extend the same courtesy when he is in need of assistance. Thus, children are socialized to be extremely sensitive to the feelings expressed by others so that they can respond to them in an acceptable manner. As a result, they are not only very aware of their social environment, they have also differentiated it (that is, they have labels for different parts of the social environment). Research has shown, for example, that when asked to free-associate to names of friends, Mexican-American children not only give more associations, but also give associations which can be classified into more categories—that is, physical, social, and intellectual characteristics.[6] One implication is that Mexican-American children may do better when the curriculum has human content as opposed to one which is devoid of social, human characteristics.

This humanistic orientation has led to the development of a specialized terminology by Mexican and other Spanish-speaking peoples in an effort to personalize relationships with others in the community. Traditional Mexican-American families attempt to make other members of the community members of their own extended family. For example, two people meeting for the first time may call themselves *primos* ("cousins") if they have the same last name but no real blood ties. Similarly, two men who have the same first name refer to each other as *tocayos* ("namesakes"). Two men who have married into the same family are called *concunos* ("brothers-in-law").

Similarly, the relationship of godparents with godchildren is taken very seriously, and it is often used to solidify relations with other extended families that have high status in the community or with individuals that are good friends. The *padrinos* ("godparents") are expected to assume spiritual as well as economic responsibility for their *ahijado* ("godchild") in the event that anything happens to the parents. Consequently, *padrinos* are chosen with great care, and the honor is accorded to a responsible and well-established couple. This couple also takes responsibility for helping to rear and socialize the child, enhancing and reinforcing the teachings of his parents. In addition, the child develops a close relationship with the *padrinos* so that he will feel free to ask for advice in matters which he may not wish to discuss with his parents. Furthermore, he can expect them to act as intermediaries in the event that problems arise in his family.

The parents and godparents of a child become known as *compadres* ("godfather or godmother; protector; friend; benefactor"); the *compadrazco* ("act of establishing the relationship of *compadres*") is the primary way of establishing ties with other extended families (other than through marriage) and occurs in religious ceremonies, such as the baptismal, confirmation, and marriage ceremonies.

The significance of close interpersonal relationships based on the extended family is often not appreciated or understood by people brought up in the American middle-class family. In the traditional Mexican community, the extended family is a source of security; the individual relies on members of his extended family for help, rather than on impersonal institutions.

Relationships between "teachers" and "learners" in traditional Mexican-American communities are very close and personalized. The teacher-child relationship is the most important aspect of the teaching process. Mexican-American children come to school expecting close personal relationships with their teachers. The "objectivity" and "impartiality" of many teachers is often interpreted as rejection. Many Mexican-American children believe that most Anglo teachers do not care about them. The teacher of Mexican-American children should, therefore, be child centered and use social rewards, such as, "I am proud of you," or "You did that very well."

Status and Role Definition in Family and Community

Since the extended family is such an important institution in the traditional Mexican community, many more persons are placed in close interpersonal relationships with each other than in the typical middle-class family in the United States. The result is that the relative position and function (status and role) of each individual in relation to the other members of the family become crucial. In the traditional Mexican family structure it is necessary that every member know his responsibilities to the others, that he know what is expected of him and what he can expect in return.

Age and sex are important factors in determining the status and role of each individual. For example, older people acquire more status due to their greater experience and knowledge of community history. Status is accorded only to those who demonstrate that they have met their responsibilities to their families and community and may therefore command respect from the community at large.

Within the family, older brothers and sisters have greater status and are responsible for the socialization and the safety of younger siblings. Parents command respect from their children but defer to their own parents, as well as to older uncles and aunts. Thus, members of the extended family who show respect for older people can command respect from younger members of the family, as long as they accept their share of responsibility for the well-being of the total family.

Two terms in Spanish characterize the main goals of child socialization in traditional communities — respeto ("respect") and bien educado ("well educated socially"). The child is expected to respect the status and feelings of others and to demonstrate acceptable social behavior by assuming the responsibilities of his assigned role. Parents place as much emphasis on social roles and behavior as they do on academic education. They are often confused when school personnel do not seem to understand that a child's duties at home, such as having to stay home to care for younger family members, are just as important as his education at school. They may also be concerned when teachers do not emphasize classroom control, or do not demand respect from their students. This should not be misunderstood. The teacher should not be harsh or brutal. In fact, the ideal teacher in the traditional Mexican-American community, is nurturant, firm, and shows concern for the well-being of the child. Discipline is maintained without withdrawal of love.

The teaching style which is most characteristic in the traditional Mexican-American community is modeling. The child learns to "do it like the teacher," and wants to become like the teacher. It is important, then, that the teacher relate personal anecdotes and be willing to interact with the child outside the classroom. The most effective rewards are those which result in a closer relationship between the child and the teacher.

Sexual roles are clearly defined in Mexican-American traditional communities. Men are considered to have more status in business and politics, whereas women have more status in religion, child rearing, and health care. Teachers should be cautious about forcing Mexican-American children from traditional families to do tasks or take on roles that contradict their sexual roles.

Identification with Mexican Catholic Ideology

Mexican Catholicism is a *mestizo* religion, representing an amalgamation of Indian and European beliefs and practices. It plays a central role in child socialization by reinforcing many of the values already discussed, particularly identification with family, community, and ethnic group (through veneration for the Virgin of Guadalupe) and emphasis on respect and social education. Mexican-American Catholicism also emphasizes respect for convention. Disrespect and rebelliousness against the teachings of parents and institutions is considered sinful. Individuals who are disrespectful, or in some other way do not fulfill their obligations and responsibilities, often experience a sense of guilt.

These beliefs sometimes lead Mexican-American children into a cycle of failure that may cause them to drop out of school. For example, a child may do poorly on an assignment but not seek help from the teacher. He blames himself for the failure. He feels guilty because he is letting others down by his poor performance. Further failure ensues. Teachers and counselors can prevent this by helping the child before he enters into this destructive cycle.

EDUCATIONAL IMPLICATIONS

On the basis of these cultural values, the following recommendations, entitled "Culturally Democratic Learning Environments: A Bilingual-Bicultural Approach," were developed under the direction of Manuel Ramirez by the Model Follow Through Project of the Cucamonga, California, school district.[7]

1. Humanize the curriculum, especially when teaching math and science concepts. ("Sesame Street" is a good source of ideas.)
2. Personalize the curriculum: relate personal experiences and interests of children to the curriculum.
3. Include fantasy and humor in the curriculum. Use puppets and role-playing techniques.
4. Encourage cooperative group work.
5. Arrange the classroom so that it permits maximum adult and child contact. A classroom with learning centers permits some children to work alone, thus enabling the teacher to work with small groups or individually with children who need personal contact.
6. If a class is too large, implement cross-age teaching.
7. Be sensitive to the child's feelings, remembering that a child-centered rather than a task-centered approach is more effective with traditional Mexican-American children.

8. Use personalized rewards which make your relationship with the child closer: "I am proud of you," or "Now that you can read that book, we can both read it together."
9. Use as much Spanish as possible in the classroom. Try to obtain Spanish-as-a-second-language material for the children.
10. Most traditional Mexican-American children need some English-as-a-second-language training.
11. Introduce Mexican, Mexican-American, and Spanish heritage materials into the curriculum. Asking the parents' help is a good way to involve them actively in the educational process.
12. Make educational materials available to parents so they can instruct their children at home.

A detailed description of a variety of teaching strategies found useful with many Mexican-American children is presented in the appendix to this section. This material, which amplifies many of the recommendations cited above, was developed by M. Ramirez, P. Leslie Herold, and Alfredo Castañeda.[8]

VALUE ORIENTATIONS OF MEXICAN-AMERICAN COMMUNITIES

In order to emphasize the fact that Mexican-American communities differ from one another, and in an effort to help counteract the stereotyped view of Mexican-Americans found in much of the social science literature, factors or forces affecting the strength with which these values are held over American mainstream values will now be described.

The relative strength with which these forces operate in a particular community determines the value orientation of the majority of the families and individuals and provides the basis for classifying them as having (1) traditional, (2) dualistic, or (3) atraditional value orientations. Some families and individuals may exhibit all three value orientations, but it is possible to classify communities into one of these three categories according to the value orientations of the majority of their families or individuals. The fact that all three orientations exist together indicates that the communities are in a constant state of flux and that value orientations can change.

In the present scheme, *traditional* communities are those which exhibit orientations almost identical with Mexican values. *Dualistic* communities begin to show some adoption of mainstream values along with maintenance of many of the traditional Mexican values. In the *atraditional* communities, on the other hand, Mexican-American values have been amalgamated with mainstream American values.

Knowing these categories and the value orientation of the local community will help the teacher avoid teaching strategies and curricula that are inappropriate for the children of a particular community. However, it is necessary to point out that the present scheme does not offer a simple or rigid model for examining Mexican-American values. On the contrary, the examination of Mexican-American values is neither simple nor exhaustive. The scheme is designed to give the reader a point of departure from which to critically analyze the impact of values that affect child rearing and teaching practices and, in turn, have consequences for the psychological development of Mexican-American children.

Moreover, one must keep in mind that any attempt to analyze human behavior (whether on an individual or a group basis) makes it necessary to adopt some generalizations. However, regardless of how many classifications or categories are developed to simplify description and analysis, it must be kept in mind that the variables (communities, families, and individuals) are constantly changing.

FACTORS ASSOCIATED WITH CHANGE AND HETEROGENEITY

The four value clusters described in the preceding pages can be viewed as forces compelling Mexican-Americans to maintain a traditional Mexican identity. They can be described as internal because they operate primarily within the value-system structure of the extended family. Now we will consider a number of external forces that operate either to reinforce or undermine the effect of these values on the individual. They are external in the sense that, for the most part, they are beyond the control of the family and are determined by such things as geography, politics, economics, and social attitudes.

These seven factors are equally as important as the value clusters because they help us understand the diversity of attitudes and values that exists among Mexican-Americans. Awareness of these factors will help teachers break away from the stereotyped views created by the media and by the published writings of many social scientists. They also help establish a conceptual framework by which to analyze the set of forces operating in the teacher's own community so she can plan better teaching strategies and curricula for her students.

Distance from the Mexican Border

In general, residents of cities or areas which are farther from the Mexican border show a greater tendency to incorporate mainstream

American values than those located closer to the border. This can be explained by the fact that areas closer to the border experience a greater influx of immigrants, who constantly reinforce others in the community to maintain Mexican values and the traditional family unit. Frequent reciprocal visits with relatives in Mexico also help maintain the extended family and the traditional Mexican value system.

The general pattern during the early part of the twentieth century was that Mexican immigrants were drawn into the agricultural sector for employment. Only after the first generation were members of the family drawn into the urban areas to be employed in secondary manufacturing industries, which were not very well developed in the Southwest. Generally, then, we can expect rural areas to be traditional and urban areas to be dualistic or atraditional.

Since World War II, however, manufacturing has grown at a tremendous rate in the Southwest, particularly in California. In the last decade, Mexican immigrants have found more opportunities for employment in urban areas than ever before. Consequently, the present-day influx of immigrants is heading directly for the large metropolitan communities, where they form enclaves which maintain Mexican cultural values. As a result, exceptions to the trend toward acculturation are becoming more common, and there are now many traditional *barrios* in urban areas located far from the Mexican border.

Length of Residence in the United States

In looking at specific communities with large Mexican-American populations, we can say, as a rule, that those containing residents who have lived in the United States for a longer period of time exhibit a greater tendency to adopt mainstream American values than those containing a greater percentage of recent immigrants.

Degree of Urbanization

The pressure to adopt American middle-class values is greater on residents of more highly urbanized areas than those in more rural areas. This is generally due to the fact that residents of urban areas have more of an opportunity than residents of rural areas to come in contact with the values of the American majority in schools and work situations and through the mass media. Again, exceptions can be found in large metropolitan areas where large enclaves exist (for example, certain parts of East Los Angeles, and the Mission District of San Francisco). Exceptions can also be found in areas near the Mexican border, where there is a good deal of exposure to "Mexican" urbanization and values (parts of Texas, San Diego, and Calexico).

Degree of Economic and Political Strength of Mexican-Americans in the Community

Where Mexican-Americans are more active politically—where they own businesses, register to vote, and so forth—they are more likely to resist the incorporation of many mainstream American values into their own system. An example of this is New Mexico, where the residents (who call themselves Hispanos or Spanish-Americans) have more of a role in the economic and political life of their own communities. Many of these people are traditional in their value orientations even though they have been in this country for many generations.

Identity with Mexican and/or Mexican-American History

If the Mexican-American population of a community or region has a strong or well-developed sense of history (normally transmitted by word of mouth from one generation to another), the pressure from the majority community to adopt mainstream values is not as effective. Normally, this sense of, or identity with, Mexican or local history is more developed in areas with a large Mexican-American population. Mexican-Americans in areas such as northern New Mexico, southern Colorado, and southern Texas (where a large percentage of the population is of Mexican descent) pass on more of a local and traditional history to succeeding generations than in southern California, where a much smaller percentage of the population is of Mexican descent. This knowledge of the history of the ethnic group acts as a buffer to insulate Mexican-Americans from the pressure to acculturate or adopt mainstream values.

Degree of Prejudice toward Mexican-Americans

It is extremely difficult to assess the effects of prejudice in a community. Where it is intense and overt, Mexican-Americans may be less likely to incorporate mainstream values because they have less opportunity to interact with Anglos. Often, a Mexican-American who does attempt to adopt new values is subjected to intense peer-group and neighborhood pressure. Sometimes, however, subtle forms of discrimination against Mexican-Americans have a more coercive effect, which results in the adoption of mainstream values. The neighborhood or peer-group reaction may not be as intense in the latter case because Mexican-Americans may not be as conscious of how these subtle forms of discrimination are compelling members of the community to adopt different values.

THE CHICANO CIVIL RIGHTS MOVEMENT

Today we are witnessing a phenomenon among young Mexican-American high school and college students brought about by the rise of the Mexican-American, or Chicano, civil rights movement. Many of these young persons developed atraditional value orientations as a result of their parents' desire to see them succeed in American society. With the Mexican-American civil rights movement, however, there has been a rediscovery of Mexican culture and its worth. Consequently, many are showing a desire to return to traditional values with a bicultural orientation. The Chicano civil rights movement has had its greatest impact on reinforcing the spirit of *familia* and *La Raza,* as well as the desire to humanize society. Most of the Chicano activists view these two values as a positive contribution which Mexican culture can make to American society.

Teachers should be aware that young Mexican-American high school and college students have developed a new sense of personal identity and worth through their own conscious acceptance of their cultural background. Now, they want the majority community to accept the fact that they can function in this society even though they maintain their cultural heritage. The fact that both cultures are seen as positive and harmonious has resulted in a greater psychological stability through the development of pride and confidence in many of the younger generation of Mexican-Americans.

Another and even more recent development, particularly at the college level, has been an interest, on the part of both male and female students, in reexamining the sexual roles prescribed by traditional values. The pertinent point in this connection is that this reexamination and evaluation is being conducted by many Mexican-American students who come from traditional socialization experiences. Mexican-American females are, with increasing frequency, running for the highest offices in many of the high school and college Mexican-American organizations and are being elected. Hence, it is likely that in the foreseeable future the aspect of the traditional value cluster dealing with separation of the sexes may undergo a more rapid change than other aspects of the value cluster.

The factors described above vary in strength from community to community. They represent pressures exerted by people (neighbors, teachers, administrators, and others) which influence the value systems of Mexican-Americans in different ways: (1) those pressuring Mexican-Americans to adopt mainstream American middle-class values; (2) those pressuring Mexican-Americans to adopt the values of other ethnic groups living in close proximity to Mexican-American communities; and (3) those operating to develop value systems among Mexican-Americans in line with rural or urban Mexican values.

The process of change, as it relates to Mexican-Americans, has most often been thought in terms of the melting-pot philosophy. According to this view, ethnic minorities progressively abandon their unique distinctiveness and in time become indistinguishable from the dominant culture. Educational policies that omit, exclude, or prohibit the use of any language but English as the means of instruction, or which fail to treat the history and heritage of minorities with equal value, status, and importance, can be said to abide by the melting-pot philosophy. Such policies serve to create conflict in children in the sense of continually confronting them with the necessity of deciding which set of cultural values are to serve as the models for identity. This conflict appears to be present even in many Mexican-American children who are partially monocultural in the sense that they speak English almost exclusively and are unfamiliar with the Mexican or Mexican-American heritage. Many such children, however, are also partly bicultural in the sense that their home socialization experiences are structured within the framework of traditional values emphasizing respect for authority, the personalization of interpersonal relations, cooperative rather than competitive modes for achievement, and similar attitudes.

ADJUSTMENT AND IDENTITY

Educational policies based on the melting pot can produce conflict in Mexican-American students. There have been two different modes of identification and personal adjustment. For example, Ramirez found that Mexican-American junior and senior high school students who identified exclusively with Anglo-American values described themselves as having many disagreements with their parents but having pleasant realtionships outside the home.[9] The following is a statement characteristic of students in this group:

I don't want to be known as Mexican American, but only as American. I was born in this country and raised among Americans. I think like an Anglo, I talk like one, and I dress like one. It's true I don't look like an Anglo, and sometimes I am rejected by them; but it would be worse if I spoke Spanish or said that I was of Mexican descent. I am sorry I do not get along well with my parents, but their views are old-fashioned. They still see themselves as Mexicans, and they do not understand me. Many times we have arguments, but I ignore them. In fact, I had to move away from my house because of our disagreements. I wish those people who are always making noise about being Mexican American would be quiet. We would all be better off if they just accepted things as they are. I just want a good education. I don't want to be poor or discriminated against.

Another group of Mexican students, who exclusively identified with traditional Mexican-American values, described themselves as having pleasant and satisfying relationships with their parents — that is, well adjusted at home but feeling alienated from people on the outside. The following statement is characteristic of students in this group:

I am proud of being a Mexican American. We have a rich heritage. Mexico is a great country which is progressing fast, and it has a wonderful history and culture. My family is the most important thing in the world to me. I owe my parents everything and I will never complain when they need me. I don't want to be like the Anglos because they don't care about their families; they just care about themselves and making money. They don't like anybody who is different. At school the teachers would ignore you if they knew you weren't going to college and most of us Mexicans couldn't afford to go. The things I learned at school were against what my parents had taught me. I had to choose my parents because now they are old and they need my help and understanding. I know most people — even some Mexican Americans — look down on us because we are Mexicans and I hate them. It is unhealthy and unnatural to want to be something you are not.

The effect of the melting-pot philosophy, then, is to encourage a one-sided identity among Mexican-American students, and in terms of adjustment the price seems to be the ability to function effectively in only one cultural world — either the world represented by the school or the world represented by the home. Educational policies based on the melting pot do not provide the opportunity for a third option — the opportunity to develop a bicultural identity, which would permit the child to enjoy satisfying relations in more than one cultural world and to identify with aspects of both. The key message of this essay has been that the philosophy of cultural democracy in education, with its implications of a bicultural approach, must be explored as a possibility for making this third option a reality. In the study cited above, Ramirez found several students who had developed a bicultural identity and reported enjoying satisfactory relationships both at home and in school. The following statement is characteristic of these students:

I am happy to be an American of Mexican descent. Because I am a Mexican I learned to be close to my family and they have been a source of strength and support for me. If things ever got too bad on the outside, I could always come to them for comfort and understanding. My Spanish also helped me a lot in my education and will also open a lot of doors for me when I look for a job. As an American I am happy to live in a great progressive country where we have the freedom to achieve anything we want. I feel all I have achieved I owe to the help of my parents, the encouragement of my teachers, and the chance to live in a country like this one. I feel very rich and fortunate because I have two cultures rather than just one.

CULTURAL-MATCHING TEACHING STRATEGIES

Nonverbal indications of acceptance

The teacher or teaching associate should communicate with the child through hugs, pats, having child sit on her lap, meaningful looks, smiles, putting her arm around the child.

She should provide opportunities for the children to work right next to her at all times, particularly when reading to them or being read to.

The teacher or associate should comfort a crying child by hugging him if that is what he seems to want.

They should be generally "motherly" with the children.

When children are having a good laugh, the teacher should not feel reluctant to share in their laughter.

Personalizing

The teacher and associate should mention personal feelings, likes, dislikes, and so forth to the children from time to time.

They should tell them things about their own life, show them pictures of their families, occasionally have their families visit the school.

The teacher or associate should treat the children as individuals. She should take care to know things about them: their favorite color or food, something they like doing, or a visit they enjoy. She should compliment them on their hair ribbons or new shirts. The teacher should also be sensitive to their home backgrounds.

Photographs of the children should be displayed in the classroom.

The teacher should know and at least mention, if not celebrate, birthdays, particularly in the lower grades.

Lesson material should be related to personal experience wherever possible. Math stories can refer to local places; for instance, mention a local store instead of just saying "the store."

Feelings mentioned in stories can be related to the children's own feelings.

Encouraging cooperation

The teacher and associate should reward with their approval instances of helpfulness and consideration that they see in the classroom. For instance, they should remark on how nice it is to see a child or children helping a newcomer to the room.

The teacher should frequently assign tasks for small groups of children to do together. Friends can cooperate on doing worksheets, measuring, playing games, cleaning up or tidying, taking messages around the school. If there is a lot of quarreling over competitive games, the teacher should try to make more cooperative activities available until the children are able to play the games better among themselves. Murals, wall charts, and similar projects make good cooperative activities.

The teacher should encourage a cooperative attitude about classroom behavior. She should point out that good behavior reflects on everyone in the room, particularly in the playground or when there are substitutes.

Whenever possible, the teacher should discuss behavior problems with the group to try and arrive at cooperative solutions to them.

Cross-age cooperation should be planned; older children should be invited to the room, and the children should also invite younger children in from time to time or go to younger classrooms to help. Older children should be used as cross-age tutors for a variety of academic activities, physical education, games, and with the puppet theater.

The teacher should frequently direct children to each other for help in their classroom work; for instance, they can ask each other how to spell words, how to do expanded notation, and so forth.

Achievement for the family

The teacher or associate should send messages to the child's family expressing pleasure at his achievements.

They should remind the child how proud his family will be that he can read, add, subtract, and so forth.

When talking about when the child grows up, the teacher or associate should mention the child's family; for instance, she could ask the child how his mother will feel when he graduates; the teacher or associate can mention how pleased the family will be when the child is big enough to drive them in the car.

The teacher or associate should send work home frequently, reminding the child how pleased his mother will be to see it. She should add a brief note to the work if possible.

Teachers and associates should make every effort to meet families personally, and to take every opportunity to express appreciation of what the families do for their children.

Teachers can make wall displays out of materials that children have worked on at home with their parents. The teacher can also send work home (such as drawings) and ask the children to bring it back so that she can put it on the wall.

Accepting the children's feelings

Children's contributions should be accepted even if they occur at inopportune moments. If the teacher or associate cannot stop in the middle of what she is doing to listen to a child, she should say politely that she will listen as soon as she has a moment, and *then she should make sure that she does so.*

Children should be free to express their likes and dislikes about activities in the room. It should be possible for the teacher or associate to say, "I know you don't like doing this, but I want you to do it for a little while. After this, we'll do something that you like." That is, the child might have to do something, but he should not have to *pretend* he likes it when he doesn't.

The teacher or associate should make her feelings known to the children from time to time, even things like moods, fears, and preferences.

The teacher or associate should be sensitive to emotional upsets the children may be experiencing and not pressure them to perform as usual if they know of, or sense, some unusual situation. In other words, a child should be allowed to have a bad day.

If a child is out of control for some reason, fighting mad, upset with his work, the teacher or associate should provide him with ways to unwind. Someone could take him for a walk; he could sit with a friendly person in the Follow Through office; the teacher or associate could get him working at something in the room, suggesting he stay there until he feels calmer.

Showing sensitivity to appropriate sexual roles

The teacher or associate should respect boys' attempts to be "manly" when they show bravery or boast that "it doesn't hurt."

She should admire girls' attempts at self-adornment ("What a pretty ribbon you have in your hair").

She should not assign roles in dramatics that children do not want to play because of sexual differences; on the other hand, if they want to play opposite roles, they should be allowed to.

The teacher should not *force* boys to join an activity that they consider to be a girls' activity, nor should girls be forced to join in activities they consider appropriate to boys. Equal value status and importance should be conveyed for both types of activities.

She should not force boys and girls to work together in the classroom if they do not want to. If boys and girls are friendly and cooperative in the classroom, the teacher or associate should not embarrass them by making remarks such as, "Is he your boyfriend now?"

Eliciting modeling

This occurs when a teacher or associate has a child repeat some word or action after her.

Modeling is very appropriate in language-learning situations for all ages.

It is appropriate in all learning situations for children of about seven or under.

Teachers and associates should have the child repeat math concepts after them in both English and Spanish.

Teachers and associates should frequently show the child how to set out his paper, hold his pencil or paintbrush, and so forth.

The teacher or associate should provide a model of how to print and how to make numbers.

The teacher or associate should provide a model of how to lift chairs, put away books, help another person do something.

In general, the teacher and associate should frequently demonstrate the kinds of behavior they want from the children.

The teacher should not hesitate to recognize a child who is attempting to do something the way the teacher does it ("Mira! You've drawn a flower that looks just like the one I drew").

Cultural highlighting

Teachers and associates should mention holidays that are celebrated by the local Mexican-American community and hold appropriate celebrations in the classroom.

The teacher or associate should bring Spanish-language magazines, books, comics, and newspapers into the room.

Mexican foods should be prepared and eaten in the classroom from time to time; the teacher or associate should refer to them when appropriate.

The teacher and associate should be aware of celebrations connected with the church that the children in the classroom will know about: confirmations, weddings, and so forth.

Mexican-Americans who are prominent in public life — sports figures, people in government, artists — should be featured in lessons and bulletin board displays.

Prominent members of the local community should be invited to the classroom.

The teacher or associate should refer from time to time to the extended family, particularly to *compadres*.

Non-Mexican-American children should not feel that their culture (or family) is unrepresented. If there is ever any confusion about which culture is better, the teacher should emphasize *differences* ("Juanito's mother makes tortillas for his breakfast, and Jane's mother makes pancakes").

Using Spanish

The teacher should be careful to use Spanish informally throughout the school day for giving classroom directions, telling little stories to Spanish speakers, etc. She should use Spanish diminutives and ways of addressing children (Migue*lito, hijo, niña)* and repeat Spanish folk sayings.

She should address other adults in Spanish in order to show the children that the language has prestige among adults. She should be particularly careful to address outside visitors who know Spanish in this language.

The daily story should often be in Spanish or at least contain some Spanish words and phrases.

The class should learn Spanish songs.

The class should learn Spanish nursery rhymes or similar little verses.

All concepts must be reviewed in Spanish.

The teacher should ask the children how to say things in Spanish.

Spanish names should be pronounced correctly.

Encouraging fantasy

The teacher and associate should encourage storytelling by telling stories frequently themselves. Stories should sometimes be fantastic.

Dramatic situations should be devised where the child acts as if he is in another situation.

Children should be encouraged to sympathize with each other and with people they hear about in stories ("How do you think Miguelito felt when . . . ").

Opportunities should be provided for the children to tell stories about pictures they draw or paint.

The teacher or associate should sometimes set up group fantasy situations; for instance, she could tell the children that they are all sitting on a magic rug that takes them up to the mountains where Juarez was a shepherd. She can tell them to listen for the sound the sheep make, and so on.

The teacher should use mood music and pictures to help create fantasies.

Questioning pupils

Rather than tell children the answers to their questions, the teacher or associate should help them realize that they probably know at least some of the answers themselves. For instance, they should be encouraged to try to spell a word according to phonics before they are given the correct spelling.

Accepting or using pupils' ideas

Teachers and associates should provide opportunities for children to devise their own activities or to help design activities the teacher has decided to do.

If a child adds something relevant from his own experience, they should try to include this experience in the lesson ("Tell me how your father knows one piece of wood is longer than another piece of wood?").

NOTES

1. U.S. Civil Rights Commission Reports, I, *Ethnic Isolation of Mexican Americans in the Public Schools of the Southwest* (Washington, Government Printing Office, 1971); II, *Outcomes for Minorities in the Five Southwestern States* (Washington, Government Printing Office, 1971); III, *Educational Practices Affecting Mexican Americans in the Southwest* (Washington, Government Printing Office, 1972).

2. A. Castañeda, M. Ramirez, C. Cortes, and M. Barrera, eds., *Mexican Americans and Educational Change* (University of California—Riverside, 1971); Thomas P. Carter, *Mexican Americans in School: A History of Educational Neglect* (New York: College Entrance Examination Board, 1970); Sioux J. Johnson and William J. Hernandez-M., eds. *Educating the Mexican American* (Valley Forge, Pa.; Judson Press, 1970); Manuel R. Mazon, ed., *Adelante: An Emerging Design for Mexican American Education* (Austin: University of Texas, Center for Communications Research, 1972).

3. Elwood P. Cubberly, *Changing Conceptions of Education* (Boston: Houghton Mifflin, 1909).

4. Manuel Ramirez and Alfredo Castañeda, *Cultural Democracy and the Educational Needs of Mexican American Children* (New York: Academic Press, 1974).

5. Spencer Kagan and Millard C. Madsen, "Cooperation and Competition of Mexican, Mexican-American and Anglo-American Children of Two Ages under Four Instructional Sets," *Developmental Psychology* 5: 32-39.

6. Manuel Ramirez, "Identity Crisis in Mexican American Adolescents," in *Educating the Mexican Americans*, ed. H. S. Johnson and W. Hernandez-M. (Valley Forge, Pa.: Judson Press, 1970), pp. 117-22.

7. An extensive description of the philosophy, rationale, research, and methodology underlying this program is found in Ramirez and Castañeda, *Cultural Democracy and the Educational Needs of Mexican American Children.*

8. Manuel Ramirez, P. Leslie Herold, and Alfredo Castañeda, "Values and the Development of Culturally Democratic Learning Environments" (University of California—Riverside, Multilingual Assessment Project, 1972).

9. Ramirez, "Identity Crisis in Mexican American Adolescents."

BIBLIOGRAPHY

ACUNA, RUDOLPH. *The Story of the Mexican Americans.* New York: Litton Educational Publishing, 1967. Historical.

ALWRISTA, T. *Floricanto en Aztlan.* Los Angeles: University of California Press, 1971. *Floricanto,* the blending of Spanish and English words and phrases, is the method employed in this collection of poems dealing with the Chicano movement.

AZUELLA, MARIANO. *The Underdogs.* New York: Signet Books, 1963. A novel of the Mexican Revolution of 1910. Provides important historical backgrounds written by one who experienced it at first hand as a medic.

BAKER, GEORGE C. "Pachuco, an American-Spanish Argot and Its Social Functions in Tucson, Arizona." *University of Arizona, Tucson, Social Science Bulletin* 21, no. 18 (January, 1950). A Study of the Pachuco language.

BALLIS, GEORGE, et al. *Basta!* Delano, Calif.: Farm Workers Press, 1966. A photographic essay on the issues of the Delano grape strike.

BARATZ, STEPHEN S., and BARATZ, JOAN C. "Early Childhood Intervention: The Social Science Basis of Racism." *Harvard Educational Review* 40, no. 1 (Winter, 1970): 29-50. Analysis of critical assumptions underlying approaches to compensatory education and its relation to minority groups. Some discussion of biculturalism.

BARRIO, RAYMOND. *The Plum Plum Pickers.* Sunnyvale, Calif.: Ventura Press, 1969. One of the few novels concerned with the exploitation of Mexican-American migrant workers.

CARUSO, JOHN ANTHONY. *Liberators of Mexico.* Gloucester, Mass.: Peter Smith, 1967. The lives of three men who helped to free Mexico from Spanish rule—Hidalgo, Morelos, and Iturbide.

CASTANEDA, CARLOS E., trans. *The Mexican Side of the Texan Revolution.* Dallas: P. L. Turner Co., 1928. A collection of diaries and depositions from Mexican leaders prominent in the Texas Revolution, offering a view of the conflict that is rarely considered by many in the United States.

COHEN, ROSALIE A. "Conceptual Styles, Culture Conflict and Non-Verbal Tests of Intelligence." *American Anthropologist* 71 (1969): 829-56. A technical report on newer modes of analyzing cultural differences in cognitive styles.

DELGADO, ABELARDO. *Chicano: 25 Pieces of a Chicano Mind.* Santa Barbara: La Causa, 1971. Selected poems depicting the Chicano movement.

DOBIE, J. FRANK, ed. *Puro Mexicano.* Austin: Texas Folk-Lore Society, 1935. A collection of Mexican legends and folktales showing cultural diversity among Mexicans and the wide compass of the Mexican experience.

FORBES, JACK D. *Mexican-Americans: A Handbook for Educators.* Berkeley: Far West Laboratory for Educational Research and Development, 1967. This concise manual could be useful to readers unacquainted with the Mexican-American culture. The discussion of bilingualism is particularly informative. Forbes's suggestions for its practical application in the school routine are explicit and directed to teachers and administrators. The bibliographic recommendations could be valuable for educators initiating cultural-heritage curricula.

————. *Education of the Culturally Different: A Multi-Cultural Approach.* Berkeley: Far West Laboratory for Educational Research and Development, 1968. A critique on the concept of cultural deprivation, accompanied by a discussion of the need for a multicultural approach and a redefinition of the function of school-community relations.

————. "Race and Color in Mexican-American Problems." *Journal of Human Relations* 16 (1968): 55-68. Asserts that the Mexican-American future will not be satisfactory unless the race problem is solved; prejudice against Chicanos will not disappear until prejudice against blacks and Indians disappears.

GALARZA, ERNESTO. *Strangers in Our Fields.* Washington: U.S. Section, Joint United States-Mexico Trade Union Committee, 1956. Based on extensive interviews with *braceros* (alien farmworkers) in Arizona and California in 1955 in an attempt to determine the degree to which they actually benefited from the contractual, legal, and civil rights guaranteed by the governments of Mexico and the United States.

————. *Merchants of Labor: The Mexican Bracero Story.* San Jose, Calif.: Rosicrucian Press, 1964. An excellent historical study of the *bracero* (alien-farmworker) movement, covering the period from 1880 to the present.

————. *Barrio Boy.* Notre Dame, Ind.: University of Notre Dame Press, 1971. Semiautobiographical account of the author's experiences as a young boy in a rural Mexican village during the Mexican Revolution and his early experiences in the United States.

————; GALLEGOS, HERMAN; and SAMORA, JULIAN. *Mexican Americans in the Southwest.* Santa Barbara: McNally & Loften, 1970. A highly compact review of the diversity of the population, its concerns and outlooks. Photographs.

GAMIO, MANUEL. *Mexican Immigration to the United States.* Chicago: University of Chicago Press, 1930. Early study of Mexican immigration by an author who subscribes to the melting-pot point of view.

————. *The Mexican Immigrant: His Life Story.* Chicago: University of Chicago Press, 1931. The collected statements of fifty-seven immigrants from Mexico during the 1920s, telling why they left Mexico and how they lived in the United States.

GARCIA, JOHN, "I.Q.: The Conspiracy," *Psychology Today* 6, no. 4 (September 1972): 39-44. A sophisticated analysis of tests of intelligence, with special implications for minority groups in general and Mexican-Americans specifically.

GONZALES, NANCIE L. *The Spanish Americans of New Mexico: A Heritage of Pride.* Albuquerque: University of New Mexico Press, 1969. The author examines the history of the Hispanos in New Mexico and discusses such topics as *La Raza,* social-class status, and the legend of their cultural traditions.

GONZALES, RUDOLFO. *I Am Joaquin.* Denver: Crusade for Justice. 1967. One of the more well known bilingual epic poems of Chicano history and heritage.

GORDON, M. M. *Assimilation in American Life: The Role of Race, Religion and National Origins.* New York: Oxford University Press, 1964. A historical and sociological examination of the concepts of assimilation, melting pot, and cultural pluralism.

GREBLER, LEO, et al. *The Mexican-American People.* New York: Free Press, 1970. A substantial sociological study of Mexican-Americans.

GRUENING, ERNEST. *Mexico and Its Heritage.* New York: Century, 1928. Valuable for its coverage of the Mexican Revolutionary era.

Inter-agency Committee on Mexican American Affairs. *A Guide to Materials Relating to Persons of Mexican Heritage in the United States.* Washington: Government Printing Office, 1969. An exhaustive compilation of references, reports, hearing proceedings, periodicals, audiovisual materials, U.S. producers of Spanish audiovisual materials, Spanish-language radio and T.V. stations, and so forth.

ITZKOFF, SEYMOUR, W. *Cultural Pluralism and American Education.* Scranton: International Textbook Co., 1969. A historical and philosophical examination of cultural pluralism.

JENKINSON, MICHAEL. *Tijerina — Land Grant Conflict in New Mexico.* Albuquerque: Paisano Press, 1968. An examination of the land grant conflict between native Hispanos and the Anglo-American settlers in New Mexico and the symbolic role of Reies Tijerina.

LEON-PORTILLA, MIGUEL. *La Filosofio Nahuatl.* Mexico, 1956. Translated as *Aztec Thought and Culture.* Norman: University of Oklahoma Press, 1963. Provides an understanding of the Mexican heritage.

McWILLIAMS, CAREY. *North from Mexico: The Spanish-Speaking People of the United States.* New York: J. P. Lippincott, 1961. One of the few references dating from before the onset of the Mexican-American civil rights movement to depict the exploitation and prejudice faced by Mexican-Americans.

MATTHIESSEN, PETER. *Sal si Puedes: Cesar Chavez and the New American Revolution.* New York: Random House, 1969. One of the first books to deal with Cesar Chavez and the movement he symbolizes.

MOORE, JOAN W., and CUÉLLAN, ALFREDO. *Mexican Americans.* Englewood Cliffs, N.J.: Prentice-Hall, 1970. A concise analysis of available demographic data with special sections on schools, church, law enforcement, and related matters, as well as political developments.

NAVA, JULIAN. *Mexican Americans: Past, Present and Future.* New York: Litton Educational Publishing, 1969. Historical.

NOGALES, LUIS G. *The Mexican American: A Selected and Annotated Bibliography.* 2d ed. Stanford: Stanford University Press, 1971. Contains 444 entries relating to present interests and concerns of the Mexican-American community. Greater representation of work by social scientists. An excellent source of original material.

PAREDES, AMERICO. *With His Pistol in His Hand: A Border Ballad and Its Hero.* Austin: University of Texas Press, 1958. The author has taken a Chicano *corrido* ("ballad") about a folk hero and examined its historical roots, showing the similarities between the Mexican and Chicano *corridos.*

PAZ, OCTAVIO. *Aguila o Sol? (Eagle or Sun?).* New York: October House, 1950. Short stories, fictional essays, and poetry by the author written in both Spanish and English. Valuable for bilingual classes.

――――. *Labyrinth of Solitude.* New York: Grove Press, 1961. A close philosophical and cultural evaluation of the Mexican character by one of Mexico's most important literary figures.

PINKNEY, ALPHONSO. "Prejudice toward Mexican and Negro Americans." *Phylon,* Winter 1963. A discussion of similarities and differences in prejudice toward Mexican-Americans and prejudice toward black Americans.

RIVIERA, FELICIANO. *A Mexican American Source Book.* Menlo Park, Calif.: Educational Consulting Associates, 1970. A useful guideline to the history of Mexican-Americans. Especially constructed for students and teachers, with an excellent bibliography of books, articles, periodicals, films, and similar materials. Excellent short biographies of a number of Mexican-American educators, politicians, attorneys, physicians, athletes, and others.

ROMANO-V., OCTAVIO I. "Donship in a Mexican-American Community in Texas." *American Anthropologist* 62 (1960): 966-76. An interesting study suggesting important values and behavior patterns in selected Mexican-American communities.

――――. "Charismatic Medicine, Folk-Healing, and Folk Sainthood." *American Anthropologist* 67 (1965): 1151-73. For those interested in the phenomena of the *curandero* ("healer").

――――. "The Anthropology and Sociology of the Mexican-Americans." *El Grito* 2 (Fall 1968): 13-26. Delineation of a perception stressing the historical activism of Mexican-Americans.

――――. "The Historical and Intellectual Presence of Mexican-Americans." *El Grito* 2 (Winter 1969): 32-47. An analysis of the pluralism in Mexican-American thought and the survival of conflicting ideologies among a people commonly thought of as homogeneous.

――――, ed. *El Espejo – The Mirror: Selected Mexican-American Literature.* Berkeley: Quinto Sol, 1969. Excellent selections by contemporary Mexican-American writers.

RULFO, JUAN. *The Burning Plain and Other Stories.* Austin: University of Texas Press, 1965. Junior high and high school students should have no problem in reading the concise, direct style of this translated work on the conditions and situation of Mexican Indians and the poor.

SAMORA, JULIAN, ed. *La Raza: Forgotten Americans.* South Bend: University of Notre Dame Press, 1966. A review of contemporary conditions.

SIMMEN, EDWARD, ed. *The Chicano: From Caricature to Self-Portrait.* New York: New American Library, 1971. An anthology examining the evolution of the Chicano protagonist in the American short story.

STEINER, STAN. *La Raza—The Mexican Americans*. New York: Harper & Row, 1969. Sensitive reporting of the plight of Mexican-Americans in rural communities.

TOOR, FRANCES. *Treasure of Mexican Folkways*. New York: Crown, 1967. The customs, myths, folklore, traditions, beliefs, fiestas, dances and songs of the Mexican people.

VACA, N. "The Mexican American in the Social Sciences. 1912-1970. Part I: 1912-35." *El Grito* 3, no. 3 (1970): 3-24. An excellent historical and analytic review of the reasons for the consistently low intelligence-test scores and academic-achievement levels of Mexican-American schoolchildren.

———. "The Mexican American in the Social Sciences. 1912-1970. Part II: 1936-1970." *El Grito* 4, no. 1 (1970): 17-51. A continuation of the preceding item.

VASCONCELOS, JOSE. *A Mexican Ulysses*. Bloomington: University of Indiana Press, 1963. An autobiography by one who participated in the political developments of Mexico. Reflections on Mexican education, history, and culture.

VASQUEZ, RICHARD. *Chicano*. Garden City: Doubleday, 1970. A novel. A saga covering several generations, originating in Mexico and depicting present circumstances in Southern California.

WOMACK, JOHN, JR. *Zapata and the Mexican Revolution*. New York: Knopf, 1968. Emiliano Zapata, the hero of agrarian reform and the leader of the southern division of the Mexican Revolution.

YANOVSKI, E. *Food Plants of the North American Indians*. U.S. Department of Agriculture, Miscellaneous Publications, No. 237. Provides information on Mexican agricultural contributions to modern society.

ZERMENTO, ANDY, and the staff of *El Malcriado. Don Sotaco*. Delano, Calif.: Farm Workers Press, 1966. Cartoons from the Delano grape strike. Don Sotaco, who symbolizes the once docile farm worker, is depicted in his struggle for justice and full participation in American society.

The Educational Needs of Black Americans

by

RICHARD L. JAMES

Associate Dean for Teacher Education
Morgan State College

HISTORICAL BACKGROUND

Throughout the history of this nation, the question of education for black Americans has been a significant part of the struggle to make the American dream a reality. In the beginning, there was no thought of educating blacks. Most of them were slaves, destined to live out their lives in servitude. The only training needed for this life was training in obedience and servility. The too proud were turned over to slave-breakers who were skilled in systematically destroying their dignity and self-respect. The slave was in every sense a tool, a beast of burden whose life was dedicated to the well-being of his master. His education consisted of what was needed to understand commands and to carry out the tasks assigned him.

Although the status of the so-called free Negro was somewhat better than that of the slave, he did not enjoy the rights possessed by other citizens. If his right to be free was questioned, the burden of proof lay on him. During the height of slavery, these blacks had to show their "free" papers on demand. Despite the fact that he did not enjoy the rights of other citizens, the free Negro was not excused from the burdens and responsibilities shared by them. Frequently, these obligations included the payment of school taxes, although black children were generally denied admission to the schools supported by these funds. In pre-Civil War America, the idea that any black could or should be educated had very few supporters. The few existing schools for blacks were private enterprises supported by religious groups and sympathetic friends. These limited educational opportunities were, to a great extent, confined to the larger cities of the North. For most blacks, slave or free, the opportunity to obtain an education simply did not exist.

With the emancipation, educational opportunities for blacks entered a new era. The ex-slave was no longer dependent on his master for food, work, and a place to live. His new status made it possible for him to have a voice in deciding his future. This new responsibility brought with it the need for education. The problem of providing instruction for the more than four million ex-slaves was enormous. In reconstructing the divided nation, this problem was recognized as a national concern. In acting to meet this problem, the federal government in March of 1865 established the Federal Bureau

47

of Refugees, Freedmen, and Abandoned Lands, better known as the Freedmen's Bureau. One of the specific tasks assigned to this agency was the coordination of the efforts of religious and benevolent societies and military agencies to provide the freedmen and poor whites with education.[1]

The Freedmen's Bureau provided considerable financial assistance to the effort to make education available to the ex-slaves. In the period from 1866 to 1870 the bureau spent $5,145,124 to support schools for the freedmen.[2] This support, added to that which was provided by religious organizations, sympathic friends, and the freedmen themselves, provided the basis for a functioning school system that for the first time made educational opportunities available to black Americans on a large scale.

The first teachers in the schools established for the freedmen were northern missionaries. However, as the system grew, it became clear that this source was inadequate. To meet the rapidly growing increasing demand, the Freedmen's Bureau promoted the establishment of normal schools throughout the South. It was also clear that the emerging black communities in the nation's towns and cities needed trained leadership. This led to the establishment of institutions that could provide training for doctors, lawyers, ministers, and other professionals as well as teachers. To meet these needs, the bureau, in cooperation with religious and benevolent groups, began to establish a system of higher education for blacks. Some of the institutions founded as a result of this effort are still making significant contributions to the nation's development (see Table 1).

TABLE 1

BLACK COLLEGES ESTABLISHED DURING RECONSTRUCTION
PERIOD (1865-70)

Name of Institution	Year Established
Fisk University, Nashville, Tennessee	1865
Talladega College, Talladega, Alabama	1865
Atlanta University, Atlanta, Georgia	1867
Hampton Institute, Hampton, Virginia	1867
Howard University, Washington, D.C.	1867
Shaw University, Raleigh, North Carolina	1865
Morehouse College, Atlanta, Georgia	1867
Morgan College, Baltimore, Maryland	1867
Tougaloo College, Tougaloo, Mississippi	1869

SOURCE: Frank Bowles and Frank A. DeCosta. *Between Two Worlds* (New York: McGraw-Hill, 1971), pp. 286-95.

In the early years, black colleges accepted their students as they were. This meant taking students who at best were woefully unprepared for college work. As a result, many of these institutions offered elementary and secondary as well as college-level instruction. Although they were authorized to do so from the outset, some of them did not award their first baccalaureate degrees until early in the twentieth century.

While the work of the Freedmen's Bureau and the religious and benevolent societies was effective in opening the doors of educational opportunity to blacks, it was apparent that a more permanent institutional structure had to be developed. The federal government could not indefinitely continue the special kinds of support and assistance provided by the bureau. The resources of the philanthropic and religious groups could not sustain a private educational system for four million people. The growing public school movement was the only answer. Unwittingly, the Freedmen's Bureau, by providing educational opportunities for many black children, created a concern for the education of white children as well.[3] By the last quarter of the nineteenth century, some type of free public education for all children had been established throughout the South. While some northern and western states had provided schools for blacks before the war, all of them joined in the movement to make educational opportunities available to all children.[4]

Although public education in the several states was established by law, white hostility toward the idea of educating blacks persisted. Efforts to provide instruction in an integrated setting were fiercely resisted and finally thwarted by a series of Supreme Court decisions that gave legal respectability to segregation. As a further accommodation to white hostility, the idea of a special kind of education for blacks was proposed. This was industrial education—instruction in agricultural, mechanical, and household industries. Among its advocates was one of the most prominent black educators of the late nineteenth and early twentieth centuries, Booker T. Washington, the founder of Tuskegee Institute. Washington, however, was not the initiator of this idea; that credit is generally accorded to Samuel C. Armstrong, the founder of Hampton Institute in Virginia. It was on Armstrong's recommendation that Washington was chosen to start the institution at Tuskegee.

While a student at Hampton, Washington had learned his lessons well. In his famous Atlanta Exposition speech, he urged blacks to cast down your bucket where you are . . . cast it down in agriculture, mechanics, in commerce, in domestic service and the professions. . . . Our greatest danger is that in the great leap from slavery to freedom we may overlook the fact that the masses of us are to live by the production of our hands, and fail to keep in mind that we shall prosper in proportion as we learn to dignify and glorify common labor, and put brains and skill into the common occupations of life . . . .[5]

In the same address, Washington had these reassuring words for skeptical whites:

The wisest of my race understand that the agitation of questions of equality is the extremist folly, and that progress in the enjoyment of all of the privileges that will come to us must be the result of severe and constant struggle rather than of artificial forcing. No race that has anything to contribute to the markets of the world is long in any degree ostracized. It is important and right that all of the privileges of the law be ours, but it is vastly more important that we be prepared for the exercise of those privileges.[6]

Washington and the other advocates of a special kind of industrial education had a significant effect on the course of education for blacks. This philosophy allayed the fears of southern whites and won increasing support for public education. Further, Washington's ideas seemed to be a satisfactory accommodation to segregation, a practice that was becoming firmly entrenched in the life of the nation. Whether Washington was simply being realistic or actually retarding the social and economic progress of blacks is an agrument that continues today.

Washington's ideas were bitterly criticized by some prominent blacks of his day. There was a running debate between the school of thought that he represented and the so-called classical-education advocates, led by W. E. B. Du Bois of Atlanta University. In the end, however, it was the industrial-education idea that won widespread support, and it shaped the development of black education until the middle of the twentieth century.

While the special-education idea was taking hold, another trend was developing that would have a long-term effect on the education of blacks in America. In the initial period of public education in the South, funds were appportioned by state law and were distributed on a comparatively equal basis. Gradually, however, as the number of pupils and schools increased, the increased tax burden became a source of complaint, particularly among those who still resented supporting schools where blacks were given instruction. These complaints resulted in the passage and implementation of legislation that made the distribution of funds a local matter to be decided by local school boards and school officials. These officials were also empowered to certify teachers and to determine the salaries that would be paid for classroom duty. Since the idea that blacks should have a special kind of education had gained wide acceptance, the way was open for unscrupulous officials to divert resources from the black schools to those attended by whites. Usually, this was done on the grounds that the training needed by blacks could be provided at less expense. By the end of the nineteenth century the development of public schools for blacks had slowed down considerably; the salaries of black teachers had fallen behind those paid to whites; the average length of the school term was less in black schools; and the per capita expense for the education of black children fell significantly behind that of whites. A pattern of discrimination was established that would continue to prevail until the historic Supreme Court decision of 1954.

The segregated school system, with its special kind of industrial education, was only part of the separate world for blacks that evolved after the end of the Reconstruction era. The reestablishment of white supremacy in the South had silenced the black voter. The black codes had resulted in the development of two distinct castes — one black, the other white. While whites and blacks lived in the same nation, they lived in separate social and cultural worlds. It was clear that they would continue to be two different kinds of people. The special education of blacks was more than just a system of separate schools and colleges. It was a way of life deliberately designed to perpetuate the racial status quo. This was the context in which education for blacks developed and to some extent continues to function.

In spite of the difficulties posed by segregation, discriminatory practices in allocating funds, and the devotion to a special kind of education, a comprehensive system of schools and colleges for blacks gradually became a reality. This system, in its early years, had two principal sources of support: tax revenues and the contributions of several philanthropic organizations. Outstanding among the latter were the John F. Slater Fund, the Julius Rosenwald Fund, and the Jeanes Fund. The Slater Fund contributed extensively to the construction of county training schools in rural areas throughout the South. The Rosenwald Fund aided in the construction of more than five thousand schools for blacks in fifteen states.[7] The Jeanes Fund provided large numbers of traveling helping teachers to provide supervision and instruction for teachers in the rural schools attended by blacks. By 1930 the separate educational system for southern blacks was virtually complete. It provided most of the educational services available to black people. Not only did it provide elementary and secondary training, but college and university work as well.

In the northern and western states, most black children attended predominantly black schools. Some states, however, provided institutions that were attended by children of both races. In 1900, one state, New York, passed legislation prohibiting separate schools. Several others mandated segregation in the elementary grades only. As the black migration northward accelerated, the general pattern was to provide separate schools. This was especially true in the large cities, where blacks were forced to live in restricted areas.[8] In the North as well as the South, blacks lived in a world apart.

The separate black world that came into being during the late nineteenth and early twentieth centuries had an important effect on the education of black people. The segregated communities developed their own capacity to provide the professional and social services that were denied them in the larger society. Secondary schools and institutions deviated from the idea of special education to provide programs to prepare teachers, doctors, lawyers, ministers, and practitioners in the other professions. Gradually, education for black youth became a duplication of that provided for whites. Graduates of the black schools, however, lived and worked in the segregated black world. Those blacks who worked in the larger society were relegated to menial and subservient roles.

In spite of their acquiescence to segregation, to the special-education idea, and to numerous discriminatory practices designed to keep them "in their place," black Americans, in the early years of this century, enjoyed a status which was little better than slavery. The violent manifestations of hostility toward them, which had gained impetus with the return of southern whites to power, continued. Antiblack riots were frequent in the North as well as in the South. One of the bloodiest of these affairs took place in 1908 in Springfield, Illinois, where two lynchings occurred within two miles of Abraham Lincoln's final resting place.[9] This pattern of violence gave rise to the protest groups that were to play a vital part in the black man's struggle for freedom and dignity.

One of the first of these protest groups, the Niagara Movement, met for the first time in 1905. This group, led by W. E. B. Du Bois, urged blacks to organize for determined and aggressive action to secure full citizenship. Among the demands of the Niagara Movement were freedom of speech and criticism, manhood suffrage, the abolition of all distinctions based on race, the recognition of the basic principles of human brotherhood, and a respect for the workingman.[10] The Niagara Movement met again in 1906 and 1907. The final meeting was in 1909, when its leaders were invited to a conference that led to the founding of the National Association for the Advancement of Colored People. The 1909 conference was called by several prominent whites who were aroused by the hostility and violence directed against black people. These included William E. Walling, a distinguished writer, whose article "Race War in the North" was the subject of much comment; Oswald Garrison Villard, a grandson of the abolitionist William Lloyd Garrison; and Mary White Owington, a New York social worker who was interested in the problems of blacks. In its first program of action, the NAACP pledged itself to work for the abolition of all forced segregation, equal education for black and white children, the complete enfranchisement of blacks, and the enforcement of the Fourteenth and Fifteenth Amendments. The organization was formally launched in May 1910, with Moorefield Storey of Boston as president, Walling as chairman of the executive committee, and Du Bois, its only black officer, as director of publicity and research. By 1921 more than four hundred branches of the NAACP had been established in towns and cities throughout the nation.

While other organizations were established to protest against the treatment of black citizens, it was the NAACP that took the lead in the struggle for equal educational opportunities. That struggle was under way as early as 1885, when a group of black parents in Arkansas successfully petitioned the state's Supreme Court for educational facilities for their children.[11] Subsequent decisions in other states provided some relief from the prevailing discriminatory practices. By the early 1930s the movement to equalize educational opportunities was well under way, with the NAACP providing strong organizational support.

The NAACP attack on segregation and discrimination in education was systematic and effective. One phase of this campaign was a drive to equalize the salaries of black and white teachers, a campaign designed to substantially reduce the disparity between the amount spent to educate black and white pupils. One of the first cases in this effort was in 1936 in Montgomery County, Maryland, where a black school principal started action that led to a consent decree granting equal salaries for all teachers. This decision was followed by similar cases in Maryland, Florida, Virginia, South Carolina, and other states. By 1950, black teachers in every state in the nation were receiving salaries equal to those paid to whites.

The NAACP also turned its attention to breaking down racial barriers in public colleges and universities. That action began in 1935 when the organization successfully petitioned the courts on behalf of a black law student seeking admission to the University of Maryland. The Maryland case was the first of a series of cases that enabled blacks to enter graduate and professional schools of formerly segregated universities and colleges.[12] Resistance to these decisions was strong. Some states went so far as to set up "instant" graduate schools in the hope that blacks would not win admission to the established institutions. Others attempted to restrict the blacks that were admitted to segregated facilities.

Court decisions regarding equal salaries for teachers and equal access to graduate and professional schools were a clear indication that the equal in the separate-but-equal-doctrine was a most serious matter. This trend resulted in almost desperate attempts by southern states to equalize their segregated school systems. As a result, in the late 1940s and early 1950s some of the best-constructed facilities in the nation became available to black children. This technique, however, was futile. The gap in quality between black and white schools was such that it would require years to erase, even if that were possible.

At the same time the NAACP had decided to attack the principle of segregation on the basis that "it was unconstitutional and a clear contravention of the basic ethical concepts of our Judaeo-Christian tradition."[13] The vehicles for this attack were five cases that started in South Carolina, Virginia, Kansas, Delaware, and the District of Columbia. These cases were carried to the United States Supreme Court in 1952. On May 17, 1954, the court issued its decision, stating that:

Separate educational facilities are inherently unequal. Therefore, we hold that the plaintiffs and others similarly situated for whom the actions have been brought are, by reason of the segregation complained of, deprived of the equal protection of the laws guaranteed by the Fourteenth Amendment....[14]

This decision was the culmination of the NAACP's attack on unequal educational opportunities. In practice, however, it has proved to be only a beginning. When it was issued, some school districts moved to comply almost immediately. These were border-state districts where the school population was almost all white or almost all black. They included the border-state cities of St. Louis, Louisville, Baltimore, and Washington. In some northern states, as well as in the states of the old Confederacy, compliance came slowly and with great difficulty, sometimes accompanied by violence. Today, more than twenty years after the 1954 decision, the nation is still embroiled in bitter debate over its implementation.

The continuing national debate on school desegregation has been accompanied by substantial progress toward the objective through the removal of legally sanctioned racial barriers in the nation's schools. In a 1971 report, the Department of Health, Education and Welfare stated that 38.1 percent of southern black students were enrolled in schools with a predominantly white student body; 20.4 percent attended predominantly black schools ranging from 50 percent to 79.9 percent black; 23.1 percent were in schools in which the enrollment was 80 percent or more black; and 18.4 percent attended all-black schools.[15] As far as the southern states were concerned, desegregation had become the rule rather than the exception. This is not the case, however, in the large urban centers, where the in-migration of blacks and the out-migration of middle-class and upper-class whites has resulted in an increase in the number of black and predominantly black schools.

Clearly, the 1954 Supreme Court decision was not an unmixed blessing. Hostility and resistance to the decision still persist. Experienced black teachers have been fired; black principals and school administrators have been demoted or released. Racist teachers are expelling thousands of black students from school for trivial offenses. Black Americans have learned that the removal of racial barriers and racist attitudes in the schools will be a long and slow process. Some have concluded that the promise envisioned when the court spoke was only an illusion. For these blacks, the new problems and frustrations growing out of desegregation suggest that blacks will be adequately served by the schools only when they have control of them. Others still see quality education as synonymous with desegregation and continue to work toward that goal. To some extent, this may appear to divide the black community. The division, however, is only superficial, for it is clear that the integrationists and the advocates of black-controlled schools have the same objective — a better education for the more than six million black youngsters enrolled in the nation's schools.

THE BLACK PRESENCE IN AMERICAN EDUCATION: A PROFILE

In its 1970 survey of public elementary and secondary schools in 8,037 of the nation's 11,799 school districts, the Department of Health,

Education and Welfare reported that 6,647,930 blacks were among the 41,456,971 pupils enrolled. The districts surveyed in the report enrolled 90.3 percent of the pupils enrolled in public elementary and secondary schools. The black enrollment constituted 14.9 percent of the total.[16]

Further analysis of the data relating to public elementary and secondary schools indicates that more than five million of the black pupils are enrolled in the schools of fifteen states. This list includes all the states of the old Confederacy except Arkansas and Tennessee. The northern and western states that appear, New York, California, Illinois, Ohio, Pennsylvania, and Michigan, all contain large urban centers, the terminal points of the great black migration that has been in progress for most of this century.

The HEW survey clearly shows the heavy concentration of blacks in the schools of large urban centers. The data show that in some cities the majority of pupils are black.

As a further illustration of the degree to which blacks are concentrated in urban areas, the data presented in Tables 2 and 3 show that the New York City schools enroll more than 75 percent of the blacks attending school in the state of New York. The same observation holds for Chicago and the state of Illinois. The schools of Philadelphia enroll more than half of the blacks attending school in Pennsylvania. In New York, Chicago, and Philadelphia as well as the other cities listed in Table 3, a substantial majority of blacks live in totally segregated communities where the school enrollment is almost entirely black.

TABLE 2

BLACK SCHOOL ENROLLMENT IN FIFTEEN STATES

State	Number of Black Pupils	Percentage of Total
New York	537,888	15.5
Illinois	413,277	18.2
California	412,945	9.1
Texas	398,187	15.4
Georgia	364,865	33.2
North Carolina	351,182	29.4
Louisiana	340,447	40.4
Florida	332,121	23.1
Ohio	291,437	12.1
Michigan	286,695	13.4
Pennsylvania	272,167	11.8
Mississippi	271,932	50.8
Alabama	268,593	34.3
South Carolina	262,974	41.1
Virginia	258,282	24.1

SOURCE: *Directory of Public Elementary and Secondary Schools in Selected Districts: Enrollment and Staff by Racial/Ethnic Groups. Fall, 1970* (Washington: Department of Health, Education and Welfare, Office for Civil Rights, 1971), p. vi.

TABLE 3

BLACK SCHOOL ENROLLMENT IN FIFTEEN CITIES

City	Number of Black Pupils	Percentage of Total
New York	393,516	34.5
Chicago	316,711	54.8
Detroit	181,538	63.8
Philadelphia	169,334	60.5
Los Angeles	154,926	24.1
Washington	137,502	94.6
Baltimore	129,220	67.1
Cleveland	88,558	57.6
Houston	85,965	35.6
New Orleans (Orleans Parish)	76,388	69.5
Memphis	76,303	51.5
St. Louis	72,965	65.6
Atlanta	72,523	68.7
Newark	56,651	72.2
Boston	28,822	29.8

SOURCE: *Directory of Public Elementary and Secondary Schools in Selected Districts: Enrollment and Staff by Racial/Ethnic Group. Fall, 1970* (Washington: Department of Health, Education and Welfare, Office for Civil Rights, 1971).

In a 1971 study, the HEW Office of Civil Rights reported that 356,836 blacks were enrolled at the undergraduate level in the nation's colleges and universities. Here, blacks constitute 6.9 percent of a total of 5,187,407 students. The same report indicates that 22,302 blacks were enrolled in graduate and professional schools. This figure represents 4.1 percent of a total graduate school enrollment of 543,150.[17] A more important factor in considering the status of blacks in institutions of higher education is the number who receive degrees. In a study completed by Charles S. Johnson in 1936, it was reported that 85.8 percent of the black students who had received B.A. or B.S. degrees in the preceding twenty-two years received them from black colleges.[18] Using data from a variety of sources, Elias Blake reported that in 1968, that figure was 73 percent.[19] Although these data are not entirely reliable, they do indicate that the black college continues to play an essential role in making higher education available to black citizens. The HEW Office of Civil Rights reports that in 1970 the (112) black colleges enrolled 158,500 students, or 44 percent of the blacks engaged in study on the nation's campuses.[20] While no reliable estimates exist regarding the number of blacks who are graduating from any level of higher education, black colleges produced about 25,000 graduates in June of 1972. This figure probably represents at least 60 percent of the national total.[21]

The HEW elementary and secondary school data show that 179,829 blacks were teaching in the districts surveyed in 1970. This figure represents 9.4 percent of a total teaching force of 1,759,650.[22] An examination of these data shows that a substantial majority of black teachers are employed in the states that once maintained segregated school systems.

A comparison of the data in Table 4 and Table 2 shows that the proportion of black teachers is consistently lower than that of black pupils. This difference is especially noticeable in New York State, where 15.5 percent of the pupils are black as compared with 4.0 percent of the teachers. Ohio and Pennsylvania, the ninth and eleventh ranking states in terms of black pupil enrollment, do not appear in Table 4.

TABLE 4

BLACK TEACHERS IN FIFTEEN STATES

State	Number of Black Teachers	Percentage of Total
Texas	12,672	11.2
Georgia	12,236	27.7
Louisiana	12,145	34.5
Florida	11,340	19.0
North Carolina	10,996	23.1
Alabama	9,452	30.1
Illinois	9,443	9.7
Mississippi	9,163	40.9
California	8,659	4.9
Virginia	8,498	18.6
South Carolina	8,482	32.9
Maryland	7,252	19.4
Michigan	7,011	8.0
New York	6,994	4.0
Tennessee	5,724	16.6

SOURCE: *Directory of Public Elementary and Secondary Schools in Selected Districts: Enrollment and Staff by Racial/Ethnic Group, Fall, 1970* (Washington: Department of Health, Education and Welfare, Office for Civil Rights, 1971), pp. x, xii.

As is the case with black pupils, black teachers are concentrated in the nation's large urban centers. Table 5 illustrates this point with data from fifteen of the nation's largest cities.

Again, the data show that the proportion of black teachers is consistently low when compared to black pupil enrollment. In New York City, for example, 34.5 percent of the pupils are black. Black teachers make up only 7.8 percent of the teaching force.

TABLE 5

BLACK TEACHERS IN FIFTEEN CITIES

City	Number of Black Teachers	Percentage of Total
Chicago	7,250	34.2
Washington	5,338	79.5
New York	4,672	7.8
Detroit	4,464	41.4
Baltimore	4,067	46.5
Philadelphia	3,718	32.2
Los Angeles	3,580	14.7
Houston	2,899	32.8
Atlanta	2,563	59.6
Memphis	2,395	41.9
New Orleans	2,374	55.8
St. Louis	2,060	53.4
Miami (Dade County)	2,018	21.2
Cleveland	1,990	38.2
Dallas	1,817	27.7

SOURCE: *Directory of Public Elementary and Secondary Schools in Selected Districts: Enrollment and Staff by Racial/Ethnic Group. Fall, 1970* (Washington: Department of Health, Education and Welfare, Office for Civil Rights, 1971).

In 1968, the Bureau of the Census reported that 5,190 blacks were teaching in colleges and universities throughout the nation. Of this number, 4,803, or 81 percent, were teaching in the South, where most of the predominantly black colleges are located.[23] The bureau reports that in the South, the ratio of black college teachers to black students was 1:18, compared to 1:28 in the rest of the country. The latter figure is probably somewhat distorted due to the fact that several black colleges (Lincoln University and Cheney State College in Pennsylvania, Central State University in Ohio, and Lincoln University in Missouri) are located outside the South.

Reliable data on the extent to which blacks are employed as principals and supervisors and in other administrative positions in the nation's elementary and secondary schools are difficult to obtain. That the number of black administrators is declining can be surmised from reports of dismissals and demotions occurring as a side-effect of the school desegregation process. It seems probable, however, that in spite of the difficulties accompanying desegregation, the majority of blacks in administrative positions are in the states where school segregation was once the rule.

THE SCHOOL AND THE BLACK COMMUNITY

Among the crucial concerns related to the education of black Americans is the relationship between the black community and the school as an institution. For many years, this relationship was a very positive one. Blacks viewed the school as a vehicle for upward mobility—an avenue into the mainstream of American society. Parents urged their children to attend school, to study hard and work for a better life. This attitude had prevailed since the emancipation of the slaves. The intense desire for an education is a significant factor in the dramatic reduction of black illiteracy which followed the end of slavery. The faith of blacks in the educational system, as a vehicle for social and economic advancement, is still evident in the continuing struggle for better educational opportunity.

However, recent developments indicate that the relationship between the school and the black community is changing. It is changing because too many schools are failing to meet the educational needs of black pupils. It is changing because too many blacks with high school diplomas are finding themselves woefully unprepared to function effectively in an increasingly complex technological society. It is clear that many blacks have come to view the school as an alien institution, one that serves mainly to prepare blacks for the second-class-citizenship role they have traditionally occupied.

The increasing hostility on the part of the black community toward the school as an institution is attributable to a number of factors. Among the most significant of these is the feeling of powerlessness — the feeling of being unable to influence the educational decision-making process. This feeling is particularly strong in the urban ghettos, where those responsible for governing the local schools often have little meaningful contact with the communities they serve and sometimes have little or no understanding of the life-styles of their students. In addition, the ghetto schools are part of large urban systems with administrative structures so complex that accountability is virtually impossible, and parents have little or no opportunity to influence the policies that affect their children.

The process used to desegregate schools is another factor contributing to the increasing isolation of the black community from the school as an institution. Before the 1954 Supreme Court decision, the school was an integral element of the southern black community. Black teachers and administrators were respected leaders. Schools served as both social and educational centers. With the coming of desegregation, this situation began to change. Large numbers of black principals and supervisors have been replaced by whites. Many black teachers have been relieved of their assignments. The limited power that black administrators enjoyed in the segregated school system is rapidly waning. In many southern communities, the relationship between the blacks and the schools is similar to that which prevails in the ghettos of northern urban centers.

A third factor contributing to the rise in black hostility toward the schools is the growing phenomenon of "black awareness." Many blacks are beginning to accept the idea that the schools will never adequately meet the educational needs of black children unless they are controlled and operated by blacks. They reject the established educational system as a manifestation of white racism and a vehicle for the destruction of the black heritage. Henry Allen Bullock attributes the development of this phenomenon to a growing frustration resulting from the slow progress in the implementation of the 1954 Supreme Court decision and other civil rights acts that were subsequently adopted. In elaborating on the development of black awareness, Bullock states:

it was among the lower socio-economic group — that assimilation first came to be a fool's paradise, and a collective readiness to seek relief in blackness was born. Black college intellectuals, bridging the gap that had developed between their middle class parents and their lower class "brothers and sisters," triggered this readiness by articulating the needs of the black poor and by offering leadership for the realization of this group's aspirations.[24]

Leading educators agree that if the schools are to adequately serve the needs of black youth, a more positive and constructive relationship between the black community and its schools is essential. This new relationship must build on meaningful participation of parents and community leaders in the educational process. Meaningful participation implies a substantive parent and community role in such matters as curriculum, budget, and personnel. It goes beyond the traditional parent-teachers association meeting, or the open-house day during American Education Week, with its emphasis usually on informing parents about school affairs. A major criterion of meaningful participation is accountability of the professional educator and the school system to the community.[25]

Concerned educators and citizens groups in many parts of the nation are already working to bridge the gap between the school and the black community. Increasing pressures from parents and other citizens in the community are forcing educators to come to grips with the complex issues involved in broadening the base for educational decision-making. Advocates of greater parental participation argue that such involvement will make citizens aware of the differences between what is and what could be; that it offers unusual opportunities to develop community education programs that will help citizens assume their new roles more efficiently. They also argue that parent and community involvement leads to a greater appreciation of the intricacy and complexity of school problems, and that this appreciation leads to a more positive relationship with the professional educators.

While the right of parents to be a part of the educational process is generally recognized, some professionals believe that parents are not qualified to engage in educational decision-making. Particularly if the parents are low-income, poorly educated residents of urban ghettos and other depressed areas, it is maintained that the involvement of such persons would compromise the quality of the school's program and endanger the professional status of teachers and other school personnel. Others see parent participation as a device that will foster the goals of black separatists and further divide an already polarized society. As the debate continues, it is clear that the question is no longer whether parent and community participation is appropriate, but what the extent of such participation will be. If the schools are to enjoy the full confidence of black and other minority communities, the resolution of this issue is essential.

A growing number of educators and community leaders see decentralization as a vehicle for increasing parent participation in school affairs in large urban centers. The National Education Association's Task Force on Urban Education defines decentralization as "a method of distributing authority in such a way as to give parents, citizens, and local school officials greater involvement in or control over the educational decisions which affect children."[26] Decentralization can also be defined as an administrative technique whereby a large school system establishes several subsystems that are given responsibility for some aspects of educational policy. These subsystems operate within the framework of the total system, which maintains centralized control over matters like educational standards and the raising of revenue.[27] Subsystems may include large clusters of schools, such as New York's Ocean Hill-Brownsville, or a single school, such as Adams-Morgan in Washington, D.C. In each case, there is a local governing board, and a majority of its members are parents or citizens of the communities being served.

Some members of the black community feel that decentralization does not go far enough, maintaining that schools in the black community should be completely separate from the central system. This concept, community control, has few advocates among professional educators and school officials. Support for this idea in the community at large is likely to depend on the degree to which meaningful participation is possible within the system as it adjusts to the idea of citizen involvement.

Decentralization is just one of the techniques that can be used to increase parent participation in school affairs. Other strategies for reaching this goal include making school facilities available to the community as a center for various social and educational services, and the use of local residents as aides and tutors. These activities provide an opportunity for developing better understanding between parents and professional educators. They can give parents a sense of involvement in the education of their children. They provide a basis for parents and citizens of the community to view the school as their institution rather than as a symbol of an alien society.

The Supreme Court decision of 1954 was hailed as a great step forward in the march of black Americans toward equal educational opportunity. Black parents had long believed that the education provided for whites was superior to that received by their children. The end of segregation, they thought, would bring an end to the "caste system" that had circumscribed their lives. Growing numbers of black citizens now view desegregation as a mixed blessing. They are aware of the fact that many black children now attend school with whites, but they feel that the price paid has been too great. This attitude was aptly described by Dr. Ermon Hogan, chief educational specialist for the National Urban League, who wrote:

Integration as a reality was as great a hoax on black people as the melting pot myth. And most important, it gave further credence to the stigma of racial inferiority because the burden of implementation was placed on the black American. Black children rode the bus out of their neighborhoods into white communities. Black teachers who were considered superior were placed in white schools, leaving black children with average or poor teachers, both black and white. Some black teachers were declared inferior and dismissed because there were no places for them in integrated schools. Black parents were charged with being unconcerned about their children's education. And black children who did attempt to attend integrated schools outside their neighborhoods experienced physical, social and emotional retribution — overt hostility, segregated ability grouping within an integrated school, apartheid in extra-curricular activities, and a curriculum designed to "meet the needs" of the disadvantaged migrant.[28]

This discussion is not meant to imply that blacks have totally rejected integration. Recent polls indicate that they are firmly convinced that a democratic, pluralistic, multiracial society is the goal America must continue to seek. However, many blacks are equally convinced that if integration is a national priority, it must be pursued on a basis of equality with all groups recognizing its merit and participating in its achievement.

The emergence of black awareness, sometimes referred to as the black power movement, is an increasingly important factor in the relationship between the black community and the school. The appearance of this recent trend toward black militancy can be attributed to at least two causes: a growing frustration with the slow pace of desegregation in the schools and in other areas of the society, and a new sense of pride and identity with the emerging black nations of Africa. James Farmer explains the influence of African nationalism on the black American in this statement:

As new nations emerged, the black man of this country saw proud black people from Africa representing their nations, arguing on the floor of the United Nations, appearing on radio and television, and speaking eloquently in English or in French . . . . The American Negro began to say, "That's Africa! That's me! That man is my brother. If he can do it so can I!" Negro groups formed and called themselves Afro-Americans. This was quite new. Never before in history had the Negro been a "hyphenated" American.[29]

This new black mood outwardly manifests itself in such symbols as the Afro haircut and the dashiki. A more significant indicator of its importance is the fact that black Americans are beginning to think and speak of themselves as black people, thereby rejecting the notion that to be called black is an insult. Bullock writes that "these changes [black awareness] mean that black Americans have begun to accept themselves as they are rather than as carbon copies of white people. They also mean that white America is beginning to accept the changes as basic conditions for the existence of a multiracial society."[30]

America's educational institutions have been reluctant to deal with the concept of black awareness, and this reluctance has contributed to the strained relationship between the black community and the school as an institution. Some educators have spoken out against black awareness, saying that it is an obstacle hindering the movement toward integration. Others see it as an endorsement of black separatism, which will result in racial apartheid. Some have referred to it as black racism. These observations all probably have some merit, but it must be remembered that black awareness is essentially a reaction to the accumulated experience of rejection and discrimination that black Americans have endured.

In spite of a reluctance to accept the idea, some educators and school administrators have begun to cope with the concept of black awareness. Under pressure from students, parents, and community groups, courses such as black history and black literature have been established. Some schools are observing special days for black heroes like Martin Luther King or Malcolm X. School cafeterias are having "soul food" days; when dances are planned, "soul music" is included. It should be noted, however, that many in the black community see these efforts as mere tokenism, designed to placate them and silence their demands for real change. Some believe that real change can occur only if the black community has control of its schools. They view the traditional school as an institution that is insensitive to the needs and interests of the black community and therefore unable to provide black children with the educational experiences they need. The advocates of black-controlled schools have few solutions to the educational problems that prevail in the schools of their communities, but their disillusionment with the inferior education being provided for their children causes them to feel that they could do no worse.

There seems to be a growing consensus that quality education for blacks and other minorities requires a more constructive relationship between minority communities and school systems. A number of efforts, including federal programs such as Teacher Corps, TTT (Training the Trainers of Teachers), and the Career Opportunities Program, have community participation as a mandatory requirement. Several entries in the bibliography to this section describe how this has been done. School districts are building on experience gained from these and other programs to develop better vehicles for involving the traditionally neglected members of minority communities in the educational process.

THE BLACK CHILD IN AMERICA'S SCHOOLS

Although the relationship between the black community and the school as an institution is of the utmost importance, it is the teachers, principals, and other professionals at the school level who must be most directly involved in improving educational services for black children. This point has been amply demonstrated by the failure of many programs that have focused on new courses of study, new standards, or new equipment and other improvements aimed at raising the quality of the school as an institution. Institutions are made up of people, and it is the behavior of people that must be a primary focus for efforts to improve the education of the nation's youth.

Studies have shown that schools attended by blacks, particularly in the urban ghettos, are likely to be staffed with teachers and other professional personnel who have less experience and lower qualifications than those who teach in more middle-class settings. The report of the HEW Urban Education Task Force cites a 1968 survey, which reports that the total number of full-time teachers with less than standard certificates at that time was 108,000, or 5.6 percent of the total teaching force. The same survey indicated a number of cities where the percentage was much higher. For example, in Chicago 33.9 percent of the teaching force had less than standard certificates, in Baltimore the figure was 23.8 percent, and in Washington it was 26.0 percent.[31] A study of teacher attitudes in fifteen major American cities showed that 17 percent of the teachers in ghetto schools had been in their positions for one year or less. Sixty-three percent reported having been in their present position for less than five years.[32] Frequently, teachers assigned to ghetto schools do not accept their assignments, and many who do, leave at the first opportunity.

These are only two of the many factors that account for the low status enjoyed by educational personnel in ghetto schools. Others include a lack of modern buildings and equipment, feelings of fear and apprehension about the communities in which these schools are located, and a lack of knowledge about the culture and background of ghetto pupils. As a result of such conditions, educators who work in these schools frequently begin their assignment with negative attitudes toward the children and a lack of confidence in their ability and willingness to learn. When these factors are accompanied by the element of racial prejudice, they become a formidable obstacle to educational achievement. As Donald Smith writes:

A teacher need not be an avowed advocate of race or class supremacy to damage the emotional or intellectual growth of minority pupils. It is very possible for a well-intentioned teacher to succumb unwittingly to thinking that children who live in housing projects or slum tenements, who are supported by public assistance, whose skins are dark or whose language is nonstandard are not able to learn. Such beliefs may cause some teachers to despair at the hopelessness of it all or cause them to engage in the curious rationalization that because such pupils are unable to succeed, they would waste effort trying to teach them.[33]

There is considerable evidence that teacher expectations have a significant effect on pupil performance. Probably the best-known work in this area is the study by Robert Rosenthal and Lenore Jackson, which was published under the title *Pygmalion in the Classroom*. Results from this study imply that raising teacher expectations about some children's intellectual ability leads to higher achievement by these children. Although the idea of lowering teacher expectations was not a part of the study, there is the clear implication that teachers who assume their pupils will not achieve soon find them conforming to that expectation. The Rosenthal-Jackson study has important meaning for the educational advancement of blacks for, as Silberman states, "one cannot spend any substantial amount of time visiting schools in ghetto or slum areas . . . be they black, Puerto Rican, Mexican American or American Indian without being struck by the modesty of the expectations teachers, supervisors, principals and superintendents have for the students in their care."[34]

Current writers in education provide graphic examples of the low expectations some teachers and other professional school personnel have for the students in ghetto schools. Kenneth Clark in *Dark Ghetto* relates the following incident concerning a guidance counselor in a Harlem school who said: "The children have a poor self-image and unrealistic aspirations. If you ask them what they want to be, they will say a 'doctor' or something like that. When asked, 'What would you say to a child who wanted to be a doctor?' she replied, 'I would present the situation as it really is: show him how little possibility he has for that. I would tell him about the related fields, technicians, etc.'"[35]

In *Death at an Early Age*, Jonathan Kozol recounts that when he asked to take his fourth-grade pupils on a trip to the museum, the reading teacher responded: "With another sort of child, perhaps. The kind of child we used to have. . . . Not with *these* children. You'd take a chance with him? or her? You'd take a group like them to the museum?"[36]

Low teacher expectations sometimes result from the teachers' empathy and pity for the students' "disadvantaged" state in life. Some teachers and other professional school people, because of their knowledge of the social and cultural deprivation endured by blacks through the years, expect black children to fail. They learn to understand this failure, and they compensate by devising special programs or activities for the "disadvantaged" child. These programs are often lacking in substance and quality. Frequently, this idea is practiced on a systemwide basis. These watered-down programs are often roads to nowhere, devices that close off any opportunity for pupils to grow and develop in the fullest sense.

Many teachers in ghetto and slum schools not only expect less, they teach less. They do less to challenge the minds of their pupils and to help sustain the desire to learn. They spend less time evaluating the work of their pupils and helping them find solutions to their problems. Their evaluations, like their expectations, are apt to be negative. When such conditions prevail, the eager spirit that all children have when they start to go to school, even those who live in the ghettos and other depressed areas, is crushed and eventually disappears. The pupil, convinced he is a failure, drops out or remains to receive a meaningless diploma.

The low expectations that many teachers and other professional school people have for black children cannot be attributed exclusively to racial prejudice. Much of it stems from a lack of preparation for teaching in schools in ghettos and other depressed areas. Most educators begin their careers with little or no experience in settings that differ from their own middle-class origins. They know little about the background of black children and the communities where they live. Even the most idealistic teacher may become frustrated when he is confronted with a life-style that he does not understand. When confronted with such situations, teachers will often show their insecurity in the attitudes they assume toward their pupils.

There is considerable evidence that children learn best in a pleasant school environment. For too many black children, school is not pleasant. Changing this situation will require the joint efforts of professional educators, parents, concerned citizens of the community, and the children themselves. It is increasingly clear, however, that the central focus of such efforts must be on the relationship between teacher and child. Black children need teachers who believe they can learn, who expect them to learn, and who will teach them.

It is important to recognize that there are a number of schools where black children are being taught effectively and are achieving excellence. Silberman describes the Christian Action Ministry Academy in Chicago, which prepares high school dropouts for entry into the job market. He also cites the success experienced by New York's Harlem Prep in preparing its students for college. In discussing the elements that contribute to the success of these schools, Silberman credits their "unusually able and dedicated teachers," who are free to use whatever materials and teaching methods they think will excite their students. Silberman goes on to say that "in the last analysis, what makes these programs, and others like them, succeed is less their teachers' talent or novel curriculum than the teachers' unshakable conviction that their students *can* learn."[37]

THE BLACK CHILD AND THE SCHOOL CURRICULUM

No discussion of the educational needs of black Americans would be complete without looking at what is taught in the classrooms where black children are enrolled. In spite of a strong national commitment to universal education, there is evidence that the school curriculum — the educational experiences being provided for pupils — has been largely unresponsive to the needs of blacks and other minorities. Recent incidents of social unrest have shown that many blacks feel alienated, disowned, and demeaned; that the educational system, through its ethnocentric curriculum, has contributed to negative racial attitudes that often make academic achievement and educational development much more difficult. If the curriculum is to be meaningful for black pupils, it must be modified so that the contributions of blacks to the development of America are no longer ignored and the black pupil can learn to understand and appreciate the cultural heritage from which he comes.

Some educators and educational organizations have already begun efforts to modify the curriculum so that it will more adequately meet the needs of blacks and other minorities. The ASCD Commission on Ethnic Bias in the Preparation and Use of Instructional Materials and the Task Force on Racism and Bias in the Teaching of English of the National Council of Teachers of English are examples of groups engaged in working toward that objective. James Banks, writing in *The Racial Crisis in American Education,* reviews several studies that focus on the effect of textbooks and other instructional material on the racial attitudes of children. While recognizing recent trends toward change, Banks concludes that textbooks still portray a world that is largely lily white. He lays the blame for this on professional educators because they purchase the textbooks that are produced. In appraising the problem, Banks states that "lip service" frequently has been given to the objective and realistic treatment of blacks in textbooks. But if such verbalizations were not merely attempts to reduce guilt, massive constructive action would have been taken, beginning with the simple refusal to purchase books that distort the image of minority groups. Major distortions of other historical and social facts are not tolerated in textbooks. If a textbook stated that the colonists had no right to rebel against the British (although a good case could be made for this assertion), the book would be on the blacklist of every large school district before the ink was dry. Yet, educators have continued to purchase thousands of books that present the image of the contented slave whose emancipation was forced on him by a benevolent Lincoln.[38]

Biased textbooks and instructional materials, especially when accompanied by negative teacher attitudes, have been the cause of many humiliating classroom experiences for black children. In his autobiography, Malcolm X tells of the following incident in his history class:

> One day, during my first week at school, I walked into the room and he [his history teacher] started singing to the class as a joke, "way down yonder in the cottonfield some folks say that a nigger won't steal," . . . Later, I remember we came to the textbook section on Negro History. It was exactly one paragraph long. Mr. Williams laughed through it practically in a single breath reading aloud how the Negroes had been slaves and then were freed, and how they were usually lazy and dumb and shiftless.[39]

Although this incident occurred years ago, there is evidence that such experiences are still too much a part of the educational life of black children. In *Death at an Early Age*, Kozol provides numerous examples of biased materials and negative teacher attitudes at work in the ghetto schools of Boston.

In recent years, members of the black community have become increasingly vocal in their criticism of the inaccurate portrayal of blacks in the school curriculum. In response to this criticism, schools in many parts of the nation have established black studies programs. At first, these programs consisted of a hastily contrived course or series of courses in black history, black literature, black music, and so on. They were taught by persons whose major qualification for this assignment was their blackness. Admittedly, these early black studies programs were established to placate the activists who were demanding that such instruction be included in the school program.

There are encouraging signs that black studies programs are gaining respectability as important components of the school curriculum. Colleges and universities have begun to provide training for teachers in this area. In-service programs for teachers of black studies are also having their effect in the improvement of these programs. In addition, a number of states have passed legislation or adopted policy statements aimed at providing greater emphasis on the contributions and achievements of minority groups.

Black studies programs are by no means universally accepted by members of the educational community. Some see the establishment of these programs as divisive, as a source of further racial polarization.

Others believe that such programs will encourage separatism and black nationalism. Despite these and other reservations that have been expressed, the conflict over whether the nation's elementary and secondary schools will teach black studies appears to have been resolved. A survey conducted by the National School Public Relations Association shows that a substantial number of school districts are setting up black studies programs or adding material about blacks to regular history courses. Case studies of some of these districts are included in *Black Studies in Schools,* an *Education U.S.A.* special report.[40]

It is too early to judge the long-range effect of black studies programs on the academic performance of black children. However, the black studies movement has resulted in an increasing body of instructional material that accurately portrays the achievements and contributions of blacks. It has promoted the establishment of extensive in-service training programs for teachers, which have not only led to the development of skills in teaching black studies, but also show promise for bringing about much-needed changes in teacher attitudes. The potential significance of the black studies movement is indicated in the following statement by Mark Shedd, former superintendent of schools in Philadelphia: "We well know that students who lack a clear sense of identity or who are confused about their heritage will probably not learn and are ill-equipped for the world of work. Thus, it may well be true that the study of Afro-American history might play a vital role in the development of a black student."[41]

If they are to be a significant force in the improvement of educational opportunities for blacks, black studies courses must be more than vehicles for achieving a strong sense of racial identity. Courses or learning experiences in black studies should be an important part of the school program for all students. Only when this is true will such programs have the potential for increasing multiracial understanding and developing more humanistic behavior. Black studies programs offer an effective and immediate means for dealing with the legacy of misinformation and half-truths that continue to impede black-white relationships in American society. These programs are an important step toward the day when adequate treatment of all minority groups will become an integral part of the educational experiences provided for all pupils. A meaningful and balanced curriculum, in the hands of teachers who want to teach black children and have confidence in their ability to achieve, would be a significant contribution toward the solving of problems and concerns in providing quality education for black Americans.

HIGHER EDUCATION AND THE BLACK AMERICAN

Although estimates of black enrollment in American colleges and universities vary, it is clear that recent years have been marked by substantial growth in the number of black students on the nation's campuses. While this growth has been reflected in rising enrollments in black colleges, it is most evident in predominantly white institutions. As noted earlier, the majority of blacks enrolled in higher education are in predominantly white schools. While recognizing that underrepresentation is still an important concern, many educators are focusing on retention and graduation as essential goals in improving higher education services for black Americans.

While the growth in black enrollment in the nation's colleges and universities is a laudable achievement, it can also be misleading unless it is examined in relation to the growth in total enrollment. Evidence cited in the *Report on Higher Education* (frequently referred to as the "Newman Report") shows that between 1964 and 1969, black enrollment increased by 250,000. In the same period, nonblack enrollment rose by 2,500,000. During that period, the percentage of blacks enrolled in higher education grew by 1.6 percent from 5.0 percent to 6.6 percent.[42] It should also be noted that a substantial part of the rise in black college enrollment has taken place in community colleges, where the focus is, in most cases, vocational. Elias Blake, in his paper "Higher Education for Black Americans: Issues in Achieving More Than Just Equal Opportunity," reports that in the period from 1960 to 1968, the gap between the percentage of blacks and the percentage of whites who had finished four years of college *increased* from 7.4 percent to 9.4 percent.[43]

Enrollment distribution patterns provide another indicator for assessing the degree to which blacks enjoy access to higher education institutions. Of the 379,138 black students reported in the previously cited HEW Office of Civil Rights survey, 264,000, or 74 percent, were in their first two years of college. There is no evidence to show how many of these were in two-year colleges or enrolled in part-time remedial or nondegree programs. Statistics cited earlier clearly indicate that the rising black enrollment is not yet reflected in the number who complete programs and receive degrees.

Access to institutions of higher education is of critical importance to the improvement of educational opportunity for black Americans. Of equal, if not greater, importance is the question of what happens to blacks once they have been admitted. Although data and information on this question are scarce and often unreliable, available evidence does support some general conclusions. For example, the "Newman Report" states that "the conflict of being caught between two cultures — that of the ethnic and racial community on the one hand and that of the national social structure on the other — forms the basic dilemma of minority education in contemporary American society."[44] With blacks, this dilemma is a serious concern, for they confront pressures to give up their community ties, dialects, habits, and values in the effort to achieve academic success. While engaged in this effort the black student has to deal with the fact that for him, success in college is not simply a matter of personal achievement. More than other students, he symbolizes his community and his race. His success or failure is also theirs. "If the national experiment in minority education is to be valid — and if it is to make further progress — educators must begin to understand what it is to *be* a minority student."[45]

One of the problems most frequently experienced by blacks in predominantly white institutions is that of the stereotyped institutional response. Many well-intentioned college administrators and faculty members see all blacks as victims of poverty, broken families, and poor elementary and secondary school preparation. They assume that black students come to them with low motivation and limited potential. Further, many see the black college student as a "militant" — a supporter of the separatist ideology. These blanket assumptions are not only damaging to the well-being of black students, they prevent the institution from responding to individual needs and abilities.

Elias Blake, in a paper delivered at the National Policy Conference on Education for Blacks, identifies three crisis points for blacks seeking success in higher education. The first crisis point falls in the period from high school graduation through the first two years of undergraduate study. In view of the fact that elementary and secondary education for blacks is generally poor, Blake urges an open-enrollment system for public higher education at all levels. Open admission, as defined by Blake, means no traditional criteria, such as a specific test score, a specific academic average beyond a passing one, or a specific rank in class. Blake's definition also applies to graduate and professional schools, for he suggests that successful college graduates should automatically qualify for postbaccalaureate study.[46]

Blake sees the first two years of college as critical. Most dropouts occur during that period. Two factors that make it a critical period for black students are: a lack of money for student expenses and an educational program that pushes out rather than holds. To meet these problems Blake advocates a financial-aid program that would free the student from work obligations during the first two years. He also urges colleges and universities to follow the black college model — taking young people as they are and doing what is necessary to give them the skills needed for academic success.[47]

Blake's paper identifies what he calls a graduate-and-professional-level crisis point. Data already cited show that too few blacks are enrolled in graduate and professional programs. This underrepresentation is reflected in an acute shortage of black dentists, black lawyers, black doctors, and blacks in other professions requiring graduate study. Because of the inadequate pool of black doctorates, some colleges and universities are finding it very difficult to integrate their faculties. To alleviate this problem, Blake urges a national program directed toward the recruitment of large numbers of blacks into graduate and professional programs. He recommends that efforts such as the NDEA Fellowship program be expanded and focused on blacks.[48] Most black educators see proposals like those advocated by Blake as reasonable and essential for the continued growth of black participation in higher education.

Frank Bowles and Frank DeCosta, in *Between Two Worlds*, list eighty-eight historically black colleges in the United States. Evidence presented earlier shows that these institutions still produce a majority of black holders of baccalaureate degrees. Many of the nation's foremost black leaders received their undergraduate preparation at these institutions. Because these colleges represent one of the few examples of black-controlled institutional life, their continued existence is essential to the well-being of the black community.

Bowles and DeCosta present several excellent reasons why black colleges are essential now and will be for the foreseeable future. First, the basic situation that brought these institutions into existence has not changed. Education for blacks is still poor and grudgingly supported. Blacks still face isolation and discrimination on the nation's predominantly white campuses. To quote from these authors, "As times goes on, and as white institutions learn to accommodate themselves to Negro students, the demand for courage for a Negro to enter a predominantly white institution will diminish. It is hard to foresee a time when it will disappear."[49]

Black colleges serve a function that is not served by most other institutions of higher education. They take poorly prepared students and provide them with skills that qualify them for professional positions in the black community and in the larger society. These graduates, many of whom would not have been admitted to other institutions, often go on to distinguished careers.

The problems of black colleges are undeniable. Many of them operate on marginal resources that make it impossible for them to make needed improvements in their programs. Their faculties are overworked and underpaid. Until recently these institutions were largely excluded from the mainstream of American higher education. In spite of these difficulties, black colleges continue to produce graduates with the skill and motivation necessary for further education and productive careers. At a time when more students, especially more black students, are seeking higher education, the black college is by no means expendable.

CONCLUSIONS

The educational problems of black Americans cannot be understood if they are considered in isolation from the other problems of our society. Indeed, these problems are national problems — not the problems of one segment of the nation's citizenry. These problems are closely related to the problems of the cities, to the effective utilization of the nation's manpower, to health problems, to problems that relate to our social and economic welfare, and to many other issues and concerns that challenge the nation's leaders. It is also important to observe that these problems do not apply uniformly to all black Americans. The black community is a diverse group with many of the ambitions and aspirations common to other Americans. To discuss the question of the sensitive educational needs of such a diverse community is a difficult task.

There are those who say that the educational problems faced by black Americans do not stem from racial considerations but are largely due to what sociologists call socioeconomic factors. To some extent, that may be true. There is, however, adequate evidence that race is an important determinant of socioeconomic status in America and that proportionately, more blacks than whites are concentrated toward the lower end of the nation's social and economic structure. As much as anything else, it is their blackness that makes it difficult for them to secure the tools needed for upward mobility. Education is generally recognized as one of the tools needed for this purpose.

There are some who say it is unrealistic to expect the schools to do much about solving the educational problems that confront black Americans. The schools, they claim, cannot make up the deficit caused by poor home and family conditions. Perhaps there is some merit in this argument. Many blacks, however, are convinced that in spite of expensive federal programs to meet the needs of the "disadvantaged," in spite of much talk about the need for understanding the "culturally different" child, the schools have never seriously attempted to do what *is* possible. Black parents have seen too many of their children graduate from school as functional illiterates for whom there is no place in an increasingly complex world of work. It is difficult to sell these parents on the idea that the schools cannot provide the basic communicative and computational skills necessary for life as a productive citizen.

Another frequently heard argument is that it is unreasonable to use the schools as a laboratory for solving the nation's racial problems. Advocates of this point of view say that schools are for education, not for social experimentation. Blacks and other minorities tend to reject this position. They feel that mass education itself is a social experiment. They are very sensitive to the fact that their children are usually the guinea pigs for educational experimenters who too often gain undeserved national prominence as experts on education for the culturally different or teaching in the inner city.

In addition, black parents are increasingly aware that the school has played a dominant role in shaping or, in some cases, distorting their social values. These are just some of the points that many blacks see as convincing evidence that educational institutions are potent instruments for social change. Arguments to the contrary are seen as evasive and obstructive—as poorly conceived attempts to avoid dealing with the complex social problems that confront all Americans.

The solutions to the educational problems faced by blacks and other American minorities must be understood as the urgent business of all American educators and educational institutions. Progress toward these solutions is retarded when minority educators have less than a full partnership in determining what is to be done and how. Progress toward these solutions is retarded when educators of the majority group persist in taking a pathological view of minority group educators and of educational institutionas whose primary mission is to serve minority group students. While it is true that education cannot solve all the nation's social problems, educators and educational institutions must play a central role in developing a society truly committed to the principles of freedom and democracy, which are said to be the basis on which this nation was founded.

NOTES

1. *Historical Highlights in the Education of Black Americans* (Washington: National Education Association, n.d.), p. 12.

2. Henry Allen Bullock, *A History of Negro Education in the South from 1619 to the Present* (New York: Praeger Publishers, 1970), p. 27.

3. Ibid., p. 58.

4. Leslie H. Fishel, Jr., and Benjamin Quarles, *The Black American: A Documentary History* (Glenview, Ill.: Scott, Foresman, 1970), p. 293.

5. Carter G. Woodson (ed.), *Negro Orators and Their Orations* (Washington: Associated Publications, 1925), p. 581.

6. Ibid., p. 583.

7. John Hope Franklin, *From Slavery to Freedom: A History of Negro Americans*, 3d ed. (New York: Vintage Books, 1969), p. 547.

8. Ibid., p. 549.

9. Ibid., p. 444.

10. Ibid., p. 445.

11. Bullock, *History of Negro Education*, p. 216.

12. Ibid., p. 229.

13. Franklin, *From Slavery to Freedom*, p. 555.

14. Ibid., p. 556.

15. *The South and Her Children: School Desegregation 1970-1971* (Atlanta: Southern Regional Council, 1971), p. 6.

16. *Directory of Public Elementary and Secondary Schools in Selected Districts: Enrollment and Staff by Racial/Ethnic Group. Fall, 1970* (Washington: Department of Health, Education and Welfare, Office for Civil Rights, 1971), pp. vi-ix.

17. "Higher Education Data" (unpublished paper, Department of Health, Education and Welfare, 1971).

18. Charles S. Johnson, *The Negro College Graduate* (Chapel Hill: University of North Carolina Press, 1936), p. 18.

19. Elias Blake, "Future Leadership Roles for Predominantly Black Colleges and Universities in American Higher Education," *Daedalus* 100, no. 3 (Summer 1971): 746.

20. "Higher Education Data," p. 2.

21. Elias Blake, "Higher Education for Black Americans: Issues in Achieving More Than Just Equal Opportunity," in *Proceedings of the National Policy Conference on Education for Blacks* (Washington: Congressional Black Caucus, U.S. House of Representatives, 1972), pp. 116-17.

22. *Directory of Public Elementary and Secondary Schools in Selected Districts: Enrollment and Staff by Racial/Ethnic Group. Fall, 1970*, pp. x, xii.

23. John K. Folger and Charles B. Nam, *Education of the American Population*, Bureau of the Census, 1960 Census Monograph (Washington: Government Printing Office, 1967), p. 94.

24. Bullock, *History of Negro Education*, p. xi.

25. Mario D. Fantini, "Community Control and Quality Education in Urban School Systems," in *Community Control of Schools*, ed. Henry M. Levin (New York: Simon & Schuster, 1970), pp. 50-51.

26. *Schools of the Urban Crisis: Task Force on Urban Education Report* (Washington: National Education Association, 1969), p. 13.

27. *Report of the National Advisory Commission on Civil Disorders, New York Times* ed. (New York: Bantam Books, 1968), pp. 450-51.

28. Ermon O. Hogan, "Racism in Educators: A Barrier to Quality Education," in *Racial Crisis in American Education*, ed. Robert L. Green (Chicago: Follett Educational Corp., 1969), p. 153.

29. James Farmer, "Stereotypes of the Negro and Their Relationship to His Self-Image," in *Urban Schooling*, ed. Herbert C. Rudman and Richard L. Featherstone (New York: Harcourt Brace & World, 1968), p. 141.

30. Bullock, *History of Negro Education*, p. viii.

31. *Urban School Crisis, The Problems and Solutions. Final Report of the Task Force on Urban Education of the United States Department of Health, Education and Welfare* (Washington: Washington Monitoring Service, 1970), p. 34.

32. B. Othanel Smith et al. *Teachers for the Real World* (Washington: American Association of Colleges for Teacher Education, 1969), p. 27.

33. Donald H. Smith, "The Black Revolution and Education," in *Racial Crisis in American Education*, ed. Robert L. Green (Chicago: Follett Educational Corp., 1969), p. 65.

34. Charles E. Silberman, *Crisis in the Classroom* (New York: Random House, 1970), p. 84.

35. Kenneth B. Clark, *Dark Ghetto* (New York: Harper & Row, 1965), p. 133.

36. Jonathan Kozol, *Death at an Early Age* (Boston: Houghton Mifflin, 1967), p. 25.

37. Silberman, *Crisis in the Classroom*, pp. 97-98.

38. Robert L. Green (ed.), *Racial Crisis in American Education* (Chicago: Follett Education Corporation, 1969), p. 178.

39. Malcolm X, *The Autobiography of Malcolm X* (New York: Grove Press, 1966), p. 29.

40. *Black Studies in Schools* (Washington: National School Public Relations Association, 1970), p. 2.

41. *Report on Higher Education* (Washington: Department of Health, Education and Welfare, Office of Education, 1971), p. 46.

42. *Report on Higher Education*.

43. Blake, "Higher Education for Black Americans," p. 117.

44. Ibid.

45. Blake, "Higher Education for Black Americans," p. 121.

46. Ibid., pp. 122-23.

47. Ibid., pp. 123-24.

48. Ibid.

49. Frank Bowles and Frank E. DeCosta, *Between Two Worlds* (New York: McGraw-Hill, 1971), p. 233.

BIBLIOGRAPHY

BOWLES, FRANK, and DECOSTA, FRANK A. *Between Two Worlds.* New York: McGraw-Hill, 1971. Part of a series sponsored by the Carnegie Comission on Higher Education, this book is devoted to a comprehensive study of predominantly black colleges. It provides a historical review of the development of these institutions, a survey of their present status, and a discussion of their role in the future of higher education in America.

BULLOCK, HENRY A. *A History of Negro Education in the South.* New York: Praeger Publishers, 1970. An authoritative account of the development of education for black Americans from 1619 to the present. While the emphasis is on education for blacks in the South, Dr. Bullock's work provides much information that is generalizable on a national scale.

CLARK, KENNETH B. *Dark Ghetto.* New York: Harper & Row, 1965. In one of the most important works of the civil rights movement, Dr. Clark calls attention to the plight of blacks who live in the urban ghettos. His chapter on ghetto schools stresses the critical need for a true commitment to quality as the only solution to the problems of inner-city schools.

COLES, ROBERT. *Children of Crisis.* New York: Little, Brown, 1964. A study of school desegregation. Dr. Coles reports and discusses data and information obtained from interviews with students, teachers, school officials, and others involved in efforts to desegregate southern schools. This work provides a good insight into the human problems that occur when social change is attempted.

FISHEL, LESLIE H., JR., and QUARLES, BENJAMIN. *The Black American: A Documentary History.* Rev. ed. of *The Negro American* (1967). Glenview, Ill.: Scott, Foresman, 1970. A history of black America as seen through important documents, many of which are related to education. Items included range from speeches and letters to Supreme Court decisions.

GREEN, ROBERT L., ed. *Racial Crisis in American Education.* Chicago: Follett Educational Corp., 1969. A collection of writings by fifteen noted educators dealing with the factor of race as it relates to education in America. Articles include discussions in the area of curriculum, teaching attitudes and practices, compensatory education, community control of schools, and school desegregation.

WOODSON, CARTER G., and WESLEY, CHARLES H. *The Negro in Our History.* 11th ed. Washington: Associated Publishers, 1966. From its first appearance in 1922, this work has enjoyed an excellent reputation as one of the best and most comprehensive accounts of the history of black Americans. Education receives extensive treatment throughout. A good source of data relative to the education of blacks in the pre-Civil War and Reconstruction eras.

WRIGHT, NATHAN, JR., ed. *What Black Educators Are Saying.* New York: Hawthorn Books, 1970. A collection of essays by leading black educators. The essays on higher education are particularly noteworthy. A good source for reviewing the ideas of black activists on the educational problems of the nation's black citizens.

The Educational Needs of
Native American Indians

by

WEBSTER ROBBINS

Doctoral Candidate
Teachers College
University of Nebraska

INTRODUCTION

The educational plight of the North American Indian tribes, from a historical perspective, has significantly revealed the inability of the Euro-American system of formal education to meet the cultural needs of an aboriginal people whose tribal values and traditions are relatively unknown to the nation as a whole. History documents the fact that the application of a medieval Christianization and civilization approach to practical education for the aboriginal peoples of North America was predicated on the assumption that it was the duty of civilized men to bring enlightenment to the less civilized areas of the world. The postulate for determining an acceptable definition for the term *civilization* was formulated by medieval and Renaissance scholars who maintained that the races of mankind could be placed into caste systems and that level of institutional achievement was the criterion for measuring a people's degree of civilization.

A Social and Religious Dilemma

Early European contacts with the tribal peoples of North America immediately created a social and religious dilemma for medieval minds whose cultural experiences were products of Renaissance religiosity and enlightenment. The problems encountered by European imperialists in the planned conquest of the North American continent caused repercussions in the diplomatic circles of the Old World, whose political relations were in chaos as a result of the fervor of the Renaissance.

In order to facilitate the prime objective of conquest in matters pertaining to the newly discovered lands, it was decided that the question of overseas sovereignty versus aboriginal land tenure would be arbitrated once the European powers had established physical control of territories on the North American continent. The legality of conquest posed barriers that threatened to lead to armed conflict in Europe and in North America as nation-states prepared to protect their vested interests both at home and abroad. The question of land tenure, where the aboriginal peoples were concerned, was secondary in importance as Europeans sought to establish their claims under the rules of the embryonic and unsatisfactory form of international law then prevailing among nations. According to D'Arcy McNickle,

European nations intruding themselves into the world of the Indians had two practical problems to solve. First, they must occupy the land and defend their occupation against the indigenous tribes and other European powers. In the second place, they found it prudent to devise procedures by which title to the land could pass in an orderly manner from Indian to European.[1]

The process of Christianizing and civilizing the North American Indian peoples began in the latter part of the sixteenth century. It was viewed by Europeans as the only means by which the indigenous peoples could be made more human and acceptable within the "natural society" of Renaissance thought. As became very evident from the onset of the process of civilization by imposition, the North American Indian tribes were not interested in accepting the benevolent overtures of foreigners who threatened tribal sovereignty by their very presence on the continent. Civilization, as interpreted by Europeans, meant that the tribes would eventually be required to give up their tribal values and mores and learn to live in the European manner. The civilizing process, it was held, would more than compensate for the loss of territory and the subsequent subjugation of the indigenous peoples. The materialism explicit in European philosophy had no analogy within the aboriginal philosophic world of nature. Cultural differences and attitudes provoked mistrust and armed conflict between the Indians and Europeans in the struggle for control of a continent that rightfully belonged to the aboriginal peoples.

Emergence of the Melting-Pot Concept

The seventeenth and eighteenth centuries found the North American Indian tribes in a continued state of conflict with their Euro-American counterparts. America, a nation of immigrants, had become a reality, and with the task of nation-building facing the American settlers, a new Christianity and a new civilization would be directed toward those savage men of the woods who lived without laws, without kings, without magistrates, and without fixed settlements.[2] Since the formation of an American image demanded that Euro-Americans "cast off the European skin, never to resume it,"[3] the words of John Adams were prophetic in that the governmental policies and attitudes toward the American Indians would reflect a need to recast Indians into the dominant Western mold if a "melting pot" of ethnic personalities was to be achieved in the emerging republic.[4]

The Euro-American version of democracy in institutions did not particularly appeal to the Indians, who had long practiced a form of democracy at the tribal or personal level. They were tribal peoples, and tribalism as a way of life was never fully understood by the Euro-Americans, whose culturally heterogeneous roots were deeply embedded in the intellectual and philosophical soil of Europe. While it may be argued conclusively that the American ideal of assimilation or acculturation is worthy of accomplishment, the fact remains that the governmental policies formulated to lessen the Indian "problem" did not recognize the worthiness of the Indians as a culturally different people. The introduction of the merits of civilization was not accomplished by direct contact with the Indians, but rather by indirect means of communication from the national level to agencies established to implement Indian policy. Transient civilization and transient education did little to convince the Indians that their salvation depended upon an alteration of the tribal way of life.

This reluctance on the part of the Indian was not ill-founded since the Indians believed that tribal homogeneity was vastly superior to the wandering life-style of the Euro-American. The conglomeration of philanthropy, religiosity, and military force that was designed to bring the tribes to civilization aided and abetted the continuing policy of treaty negotiation and tribal removal, in the steadfast belief that savagery would recede while civilization spread its influence over the entire continent in order that manifest destiny might become reality.[5] The American intent was obvious: to civilize the Indians, with or without their consent, while neglecting to foresee the consequences of these actions. Governmental policies, implemented on a basis of both expediency and ignorance, were doomed to failure. Legislative acts could not, and would not, account for the negative consequences of Indian-white relations: the breakdown of tribal society, the failure of the civilizing program to lead to the incorporation of the Indians into the white man's world, and the steadfast refusal of many Indians to take the final step into civilization.[6]

The Ambiguity of Official Indian Policies

Indian policy throughout the years has created a myriad of problems for both Indian and non-Indian alike since legislation has failed to create a common goal in terms of human understanding and the improvement of relations between the tribes and their governmental benefactors. The basic premise for initiating an Indian policy was a contradiction in itself. Indian policy was intended to exclude Indians from national life[7] while at the same time replacing Indian cultures with the habits and values of Western culture.[8]

In order to bring the tribes to a state of civilization acceptable to Euro-Americans, the process of Christian education was implemented. It typified the agrarian approach to the salvation of the Indians. The curriculum consisted of religion, farming, homemaking, and the three R's.[9] The dismal failure of the early schools for Indians resulted in a few individuals surviving the programs, and those who survived usually left their tribal groups.[10] Education as a discipline had very little impact, whether on the reservations or wherever the Indian tribes might be located.[11] While the responsibility for administering Indian affairs was vested in the Congress of the United States, whose yearly appropriations determined the extent of civilizing to be done in any given fiscal year, the enormous task of bringing the Indians into the mainstream of American society was divided between government and religious organizations. Monies allocated for Indian education were turned over to religious organizations to supplement funds already expended by various denominations in providing the Christian education thought to be so vital for proper civilization.

Indian participation in determining the efficacy of agrarian and religiously oriented educational programs was not thought necessary or practical, for there were few Indians whose knowledge of governmental operations was considered to be adequate to offer solutions to the perplexing problems faced by both Indians and policymakers. Civilized Indians were few in number, and their abilities were not utilized in attempting to bridge the gap between Indian goals and objectives, as seen from the tribal viewpoint, and the goals and objectives of the officials entrusted with implementing the government's Indian policy. It soon became apparent to the Indians, because of the ambiguity of governmental policy, that the political structure of America was not intended to enhance tribal well-being and that the price paid for civilization would, indeed, be tremendous.

Failure of Official Indian Policy

Eighteenth-century Indian policy failed to achieve the intended results of making the tribal peoples self-sufficient, participating members of the growing American society. The continuation of tribal removal and encroachment on Indian lands marked the inconsistency of an Indian policy supposedly enacted to insure tribal sovereignty in America. The combination of broken treaties and mismanagement of Indian affairs further alienated the Indian peoples to the notion that assimilation into the mainstream of American society was in their best interests. As the American frontier extended westward, the situation that faced Indian tribes in the East was repeated time and time again, with the prairie tribes feeling the adverse effects of the civilizing process that came by wagon train and riverboat.

Congressional appropriations to manage the affairs of the prairie tribes that came under the jurisdiction of the embryonic Bureau of Indian Affairs after the Civil War era reflected a concern for the acceleration of educational programs for the Indians. The educational objectives for disenfranchised tribes remained agrarian even as the agricultural frontier overwhelmed the lands once set aside exclusively for Indian use. The necessity for remaking the Indians in the image of the white farmer of rural America[12] was given full congressional approval by an appropriation of $100,000 for the establishment and maintenance of federal industrial schools in 1870.

The development of a reservation school system, administered by missionary personnel and supported by federal funds, was further complicated by the establishment of off-reservation schools, such as Carlisle Institute in Pennsylvania, which gave added impetus to the belief that daily tribal affiliation was detrimental to the educational welfare of Indian children. Removal of the children from their native environment at a very early age and subjecting them to American values and mores in a boarding-school situation were deemed both necessary and humane elements in the character development of Indians, for tribal affiliations were considered to be morally and intellectually inferior.

Farming operations, homemaking, and the three R's constituted the Christian educational curriculum after 1870. While the agrarian approach to the "civilizing" of the North American Indians continued to a failure in terms of academic and vocational achievement, it was successful in accomplishing the gradual destruction of the social, political, economic, and religious aspects of tribal living. Indians refused to become farmers after the rural American image, and their lack of desire for agrarian education was reflected in the low level of achievement, which averaged two years or less. To facilitate the civilizing process in the school systems and assure success in the teaching of English, Indian children were forbidden to speak their native languages. The federal government assumed more responsibility for the education of its Indian "wards" by appropriating additional funds to supplement the operations of both mission schools and boarding facilities, through the philosophies and methodology of which the civilizing of the Indian would be achieved.

The Educational System—Paternalistic Imposition

The development of educational institutions to meet the needs of an agrarian society and to nurture the agrarian philosophy essential to the task of nation-building was ideally suited to the emerging American way of life. The essence of nation-building and the formation of a philosophy of life were of lesser concern to the Indians, whose aboriginal world was being destroyed within their lifetimes. Educational systems and institutions meant little to the Indians, for their physical and psychological well-being was being threatened, and they were filled with apprehension concerning the uncompromising future. Forced and paternalistic imposition of foreign values and philosophies did nothing to encourage the tribes to accept the American way of life bestowed upon them by benevolent organizations and self-righteous individuals.

The statement of the great Kiowa leader and orator, Satanta, at the Medicine Lodge Council in 1867 was an indictment of the profound misunderstanding of the Indians by their non-Indian "friends." In simple but telling words, Satanta spoke for all Indians.

> I love the land and the buffalo and will not part with it. I want you to understand well what I say. Write it on paper. . . . I hear a great deal of good talk from the gentlemen whom the Great Father sends us, but they never do what they say. I don't want any of the medicine lodges schools and churches within the country. I want the children raised as I was. . . .[13]

The cultural dilemma prevailing on the established Indian reservations and quasi-territories mirrored the traumatic existence of America's aboriginal population, who asked only to be left alone to work out a new life for themselves within the context of their tribal origins. Fully realizing that the Euro-American majority would reduce tribal sovereignty to mere islands of cultural isolation, American Indian leaders attempted again and again, at the negotiating table and on the field of battle, to buy time for their respective tribes, hoping that if they eventually became civilized this might insure them the right to self-determination. However, the Euro-American, who was the product of a heritage that spanned four thousand years of cultural development, expected immediate results from the Indian, who had been in contact with that culture for barely one hundred years. Indeed, the Indian was required, by statutory law enacted in Congress assembled, to become an Anglo-Saxon with agrarian characteristics almost overnight. Needless to say, the Indians rejected the benevolent destiny so generously bestowed upon them without their consent, and they remained themselves, much to the chagrin of their puzzled benefactors.

In attempting to understand their situation with regard to total governmental control over their lives, the Indians seldom found reasons to hide their indifference to the events that were occurring all around them in the name of civilization and Christianity. While outwardly displaying some benign interest in certain aspects of the revised tribal way of life, inwardly the Indians were subtly rejecting the various programs of assimilation by the only means available to them: passivity and silence. Even Indians who sought to understand the logic and utility of the American conception of ethnic assimilation could not comprehend the need for educational and cultural programs that deemphasized Indianness and subjected children to forced removal from their families. The by-products of the developing American society—that is, material comforts—were utilized by the Indians as gifts and novelties and used for exchange purposes within the tribal societies, but the adaptation by Indians to the style and gadgetry of modern America in no way implied that civilization and Christianization approaches were the motivating factors behind the cultural exchange. The manipulation of environment as an individual prerogative rather than mass acceptance of socioeconomic demands marked the Indian dimension of social theory.

The failure of governmental and religious organizations to civilize the American Indians to "fit" the dominant Western mold has been attributed to any number of factors, with much criticism being leveled at the Indians for their reluctance to be whitewashed, as it were. The observations and inferences that determine American Indian policy are not based on revelations by Indians about themselves, but rather on an academic and political knowledge of Indians for which there is little, if any, scientific basis. The twentieth century heralded a new beginning for modern America, but for the American Indian the policies and institutions remained the same. The federal government, by continuing its policy of cultural isolation, failed to attain its implied goal of life, liberty, and the pursuit of happiness for the Indians.

THE FUTILITY OF THE RESERVATION SYSTEM

A boy about ten years of age was brought to the mission school by his parents. Like most Indian parents they were inordinately proud of this little fellow and so dressed him for the occasion. His face was painted, he wore a decorated skin shirt, beaded leggings, and moccasins. His carefully braided hair was set off by a few eagle feathers and in his hand he carried a fine pipe with a decorated stem, to use in praying to the pagan powers in whom he had been taught to trust. He stood erect, with a fearless proud look.[14]

Disappearance of Authentic Forms of Indian Culture

For over three hundred years the North American Indian has been the reluctant recipient of a contrived social, political, economic, and religious disruption that has been visited upon him in the name of Euro-American civilization and Christianity. The imposition of the tenets of a foreign culture forcibly altered the original tribal norms to such an extent that there are no longer any authentic forms of the ancient Indian cultures among any of the tribes of North America. With or without their consent, the Indians were forced to coexist with the encroaching Euro-Americans, whose philosophy of self-government and self-determination precluded any notion of aboriginal rights and tenure.

The acceleration of social and environmental change weighed heavily in favor of the Euro-American emigrants, and their prime ambition was to secure a continent and to establish a way of life for themselves that they had not known previously in a Europe seething with social chaos. With the establishment of what has come to be known as the American way of life, the original inhabitants of this land were herded into areas known as reservations and left to languish as relics of an unknown age and era. As the reservation system of human logistics gradually became entrenched, with a new and foreign philosophy of life as a model, the vestiges of ancient aboriginal beliefs, customs, and tradition played less and less of a role in the lives of the tribal peoples.

Congressional legislation, bolstered by a superficial knowledge of the Indians acquired on the frontier, and combined with a religious, philanthropic motivation, created and promoted a reservation style of life that was neither American in its philosophy nor Indian in its orientation. While the rest of American society was progressing through the stages of agrarian and technological development, the American Indians were being given medieval religious and moral training that had no practical value in meeting the challenges of cultural change. Consequently, the rules and regulations legislated by the Congress, pertaining solely to the Indians and supposedly for their benefit, legally contained the ways and means by which the aboriginal cultures were destroyed. In place of the self-sufficient aboriginal cultures of the past, there evolved a culturally unique reservation welfare state. The implementation of America's Indian policy gradually institutionalized benign paternalism as the answer to the newly created social problems encountered by all the tribes as a result of the loss of Indian self-determination.

Legislated Destiny—Ineptitude in Handling Indian Affairs

Modern America's total ignorance of the American Indian's frustration with a legislated destiny mirrors the nation's indifference to the plight of reservation people. The actions, deeds, and promises resulting from Indian political and social confrontation with governmental officials at the agency outposts and at the national level of Indian administration reflect the historic and symbolic cycle of pacific gestures that have come to epitomize the ineptitude institutionalized in Indian affairs. Historical actualities, coupled with cultural platitudes, have formed the basis for a politically unique, morally unethical, and culturally retrogressive legal patronage, and yet the "blankets-for-land" approach to solving the social dilemma of the American Indian continues unquestioned and unexamined. It is inconceivable that an agency of the national government, the Department of the Interior, whose primary function is to oversee national physical resources, should continue to be entrusted with the administration of the total human needs of the American Indian people.[15]

Indian affairs are an integral part of the larger national government, and the priority given Indian cultural needs within the framework of federal administration can be measured by the fact that Indian affairs are entrusted to a department which has legal jurisdiction for the safeguarding of America's natural resources. The alienation of American Indians from the rest of American society should not be interpreted as implying that the Indians are totally responsible for their predicament. Under the present system of human logistics that comprises the reservation system, the United States government has created and monetarily maintained a contrived culture specifically for the Indians as a means of social control and for bringing the tribes to civilization. The reservation system is the only noncreative method for constructive social change that has been initiated by the government in attempting to solve the problems brought about by a state of benign and legalized paternalism. The socializing and Christianizing processes have had one goal or objective, and that is to remake the Indian into a nonidentifiable human entity. Despite Indian resistance to legislated acculturation and assimilation, a cultural evolution has taken place that further threatens to alienate tribal people from the rest of contemporary American society.

The cultural evolution and its impact on reservation people is currently evidenced by vocal and political activism both on and off the reservation. This activism attempts to explain the current Indian social dilemma by an oversimplification of historical actualities, and seeks to find answers by defending certain generalizations about the Indian system of values. The question that must be answered is simply this: Are the values that contemporary Indians are so reluctant to part with the same values that created the powerful aboriginal sovereign nations of the past? It is quite possible that real answers to the real problems that face contemporary American Indians will be found in a total examination of what passes for Indian culture today, as opposed to what constituted aboriginal culture in the past. It must be remembered that the reservation system, per se, was a legislated environment in which foreign values were taught to the Indians in order to prepare them to become participating members of the larger American society. The imposition of a foreign set of values upon the Indian peoples of the past, whose own set of values allowed them to be self-sufficient in a more natural environment, has created a somewhat false set of values appropriate to the reservation lifestyle, which was not intended to be Indian in orientation.

Pseudoculture Has Developed on the Reservations

To alleviate the problems that will challenge the American Indian in a highly technological and industrial society, the search for answers to the reservation social dilemma must begin by a close examination of the aboriginal heritage and culture in all their stages of progressive development, up to and including the institutionalization of the reservation system in America. At the same time Indian people must make a concerted effort to provide a frame of reference whereby Indian cultural traits are determined to be authentic, rather than misrepresentations adopted to fit the role the Indians were expected to play and thus give credibility to the reservations system of cultural destruction.

The present emphasis on promulgating the values attributed to Indians, which has largely been developed by non-Indians in order to provide some workable methodology for bringing the Indians out of their cultural dilemma, would be considered worthy if not for the fact that such an approach is detrimental to the physical and psychological well-being of the Indian people. In view of the fact that the observations and inferences made thus far have used the reservation culture as the model for inferring the values that have supposedly governed the tribes from time immemorial, it is highly doubtful whether much credence should be given to the values currently being expounded upon as peculiarly Indian in orientation. Little, if anything, is ever written about the effect of the stultifying reservation system upon the prereservation values of American Indians, yet the current Indian cultural perspective is largely a product of the reservation. Genuine Indianness, to all intents and purposes, can never be totally comprehended or defined since the multitudinous facets of the old or ancient aboriginal gestalt has been lost to history. At best, what with the obliteration of the ancient way of life by legal decree, enforced by military action and encouraged by the religiosity and naive philanthropy of the American frontier era, there exists only a rough facsimile of aboriginality on the reservations and in Indian communities.

Historically, the reservations were established as permanent land areas set aside for the exclusive use of the Indian tribes. The rules and regulations pertaining to reservation lands and reservation people were formulated by the United States government, and it was clearly intended that the Indian tribes would not be allowed to develop their own paths to cultural progress. Acculturation and assimilation formed the basis for American Indian policy, which was strictly enforced by governmental agencies, and the ensuing years of cultural attrition gradually erased the last vestiges of authentic aboriginal culture as it had been practiced in a natural environment. The social and psychological effect of the loss of the individual freedoms that were an inherent part of previous Indian cultures gradually set the stage for the development of the present Indian way of life.

Thus, if the present Indian way of life can be said to be contrived, in seeking to present an argument which offers new insight into the complexities that surround the Indian cultural dilemma, it must necessarily follow that both Indians and non-Indians are unconsciously aiding and abetting the eradication of the primary strengths that were once a vital part of aboriginal cultures.

Self-Determination for the Tribes

The present social and political activism of American Indians emphasizes the need for nongovernmental interference in all aspects of Indian affairs. Indian self-government is predicated on the assumption that there can be "self-determination without termination." This statement of purpose is both contradictory and self-defeating when viewed in the larger context of the structure of political and social realities. As interpreted by prereservation tribal societies, self-determination was a reality constantly reinforced by the daily use of innate human abilities in overcoming the harsh and uncompromising challenges of a natural environment. The survival of entire peoples depended on the active participation of each tribal individual, and personal worth depended on personal responsibility in the maintenance of tribal self-sufficiency.

In contrast to the previous way of Indian life, the present Indian social and political pronouncement of "self-determination without termination" implies only a change in the leadership or administrative personnel from time to time, while maintaining the reservation status quo of dependency on less than benevolent congressional appropriations. Since independence and dependence constitute separate realities, tribal independence cannot be predicated on a form of dependence if self-determination is the Indian social and political goal.

The reality of self-determination will require a general and reflective comparison of past and present Indian ways of life. In the final analysis, this may reveal incredible and perhaps incompatible philosophical differences between the original value orientation and the reservation set of values. A genuine pattern of Indian values must be established, based on a philosophy of life that sees each individual as responsible for making all tribal people producers instead of mere consumers of the benefits of tribal social, political, and economic endeavors. Self-determination as a social, political, and economic goal would command total responsibility of the individual tribal member to the development of a way of life that will spare future generations the agony and despair of the present cultural conflict.

There are no systematically developed guidelines for the proper study of the aboriginal and modern American Indian gestalts. In the past the stereotypes of American Indians and "Indianness" were derived from the writings of non-Indians, whose actual knowledge of aboriginal people and their folkways was hindered by the lack of the language skills and academic backgrounds so necessary for understanding or recognizing obvious or subtle actions of people who lived a tribal way of life. More often than not, the observer, studying and interacting with a homogeneous community of people, was further hindered by his physical and philosophical frame of reference, which was totally heterogeneous in disposition. From the earliest writings of non-Indian authors, and up to and including the present authoritative historians and researchers, the general characteristics attributed to the American Indian have been derived from a historical approach based on attempts to understand and interpret the life-style of the modern tribes.

This methodology has been accepted as valid because there is little inclination to develop a more comprehensive study and because an abundance of materials supports the preconceived theories about the Indians. What has been forgotten, apparently, is the fact that all human societies, regardless of their stage of development on the scale of cultural progress, have their own philosophers, sociologists, politicians, psychologists, artists, economists, educators, musicians, theologians, doctors of medicine, scientists, and historians, no matter how primitive when judged by today's social and technological standards. In the case of America's only indigenous people, however, we suffer from an almost total lack of knowledge of the original Indian societal structure.

The Failure of a Contrived Culture

The social, political, and economic approach to solving the cultural dilemma of today's Indian population is without analogy in American history. The failure of the government to recognize the incredibility of attempting to initiate and devise a programmed destiny that both defies and reverses the innate order of human nature is only paralleled by Indians' acceptance of a contrived culture that has become a legal and moral justification for continued governmental administration of Indian affairs. It is ironic that neither the federal government nor the Indians are fully cognizant of the futility of trying to alleviate tribal problems by the use of imposed solutions.

To solve the social problems of a contrived culture, one can only resort to the use of contrived solutions that seldom, if ever, evolve past the hypothetical stage. If the present Indian culture bore a close resemblance to previous Indian cultures, at least in its values, perhaps the massive programs designed to provide an orientation of sorts into the complexities of an industrialized and technological society might well have been successful. As it is, there appears to be no common ground on which to build a foundation of cultural progress, for there is no common recognition of the problem to be solved. To further complicate the problem, there is little doubt that the present Indian way of life is for real, and some means must now be found to utilize the years of cultural attrition as an example of unethical procedure in legislated social change.

There is no moral or ethical justification for the total obliteration of an aboriginal culture. Political and economic expediency are no excuse. In effect, the very arguments used in the last century to justify placing the tribes on the reservations are now being refined to a new degree of subtlety, and it is claimed that the Indians are being socially, politically, and economically sustained as evidence of American goodwill and atonement for the injustices of the past.

Indian acceptance of this goodwill and the many forms of restitution has produced no constructive social progress, in part, at least, because of the lack of knowledge of the immediate social environment and its effect on the reservation people. While numerous studies purport to explain the Indian dilemma in terms of modern social, educational, and anthropological theory, the fact remains that for reservation people, the more things change, the more they remain the same. If the American Indians have conformed to the cultural mold that was made for them, the research materials being produced about them must be of questionable social value.

Deficiencies in Modern Methods of Indian Studies and Research

In terms of actual knowledge of Indians and the forces shaping the Indian view of the world, few individuals, if any, have personal access to the intimate thoughts and philosophies of the tribal peoples of North America. Through the use of observation and of inference from existing modes of tribal cultural development, there has evolved a less than accurate conception of Indian values, which, if believed, would insure the polarization and alienation of Indians from the rest of American society. In short, the scholars whose expertise is the study of aboriginal Americans have well documented certain cultural habits or traits that exist among reservation people. However, any individual — regardless of race, color, creed, or national origin — would exhibit similar traits or habits after a few generations of reservation living in which all the important facets of his culture were legislated out of existence.

Thus, scientific documentation should not be construed to mean that inferences and observations about the present-day Indians are valid in a linear, historical sense. An in-depth study of ancient tribal cultural progress and development from prehistoric times to the inception of the modern reservation pattern of culture would be in order to substantiate the cultural and behavioral traits presently accepted as peculiarly Indian in practice and orientation. In the examination of Indian societies past and present, what now passes for expertise in describing the peculiar lot of modern-day Indians can be attributed to a knowledge of what has historically transpired in the more recent past, rather than a more detailed examination of the dynamics of cultural evolution over a greater and extended period of time.

The available materials describing the cultural-value conflicts of American Indians when contrasted to the American Protestant ethic both provide and reinforce a continuity of Indian and non-Indian social conflict. As long as the enigma of supposedly contrasting social patterns provides the background for maintaining a state of benign paternalism as the means for resolving cultural problems, the American Indian societies will never achieve any semblance of self-determination and self-sufficiency.

Obviously, such statements as the "overflowing hordes of non-Indians, their materialistic economic system, and their exploitive attitude toward nature (land, buffalo, trees, deer) made it impossible for the historic Indian social and economic system to continue"[16] are gross misrepresentations of historical fact, and lend themselves to an oversimplification of the innate abilities of groups of people that utilized their natural environment to develop unique and viable cultures. This example of subtle inference can be, and has too often been, construed to mean that the "historic Indian social and economic system" contained no practical qualities worthy of serious consideration. Such qualified and questionable generalizations have not adequately been challenged by the Indian or non-Indian community in seeking answers to the present reservation cultural dilemma.

General acceptance of the way American Indians are, as opposed to the way aboriginals were, is qualified by any review of literature pertaining to tribal people. The Indian, as Margaret Mead has pointed out, has tenaciously clung to many customs and traditional views which do not encompass the folkways required in an industrial and postindustrial society.[17] This is another example of the nondifferentiation and nonrecognition of the contrived modern American Indian culture in contrast to the aboriginal cultures of the past. Present and future researchers must be cognizant of the fact that the Indian culture that exists on the reservations and in present-day Indian communities is a rough facsimile of an aboriginal way of life that was destroyed in the name of Christianity and civilization. In retrospect, perhaps the qualities that gave rise to the aboriginal cultures in the almost forgotten past would be worthy components in sustaining modern

American Indians who live in a technological society. Today's researchers must acknowledge and recognize the existence of the separate cultural realities that now comprise the American Indian gestalt.

Indians Forced into an Ambiguous Social Framework

Stuart Chase observes that the first task of every human society parallels the first task of all other living creatures — namely, to adjust to the environment and survive.[18] Confinement of the American Indians on reservations brought about an end to the era of true aboriginality that had existed on the continent of North America for thousands of years. With confinement there came an adaptation of former tribal needs and functions to coincide with the life-style of benign dependency initiated and enforced by the American government. The Indians were led to believe, by treaty and by congressional legislation, that their cultural and territorial capitulation would someday be compensated by the American people and the national government. Compensation did come eventually, but in the form of a way of life that neither encompasses the vestiges of aboriginal self-sufficiency nor emulates the American belief in self-determination of the individual.

Within this ambiguous framework of legislated human reference, the American Indians have developed a new culture that fits the immediate environment of the reservation, and consequently they are redeveloping and adapting their habits and customs to reinforce certain misconceptions that some have come to believe about themselves. More often than not, what American Indians have come to believe about themselves contradicts, at least to some extent, what is known about the basic tenets of past and present societies of men regardless of their cultural origin. Nowhere in the annals of aboriginal American history can we find a parallel to the unique life-style of the Americanized Indian that is seen on the reservations of today.

This is so for the simple reason that such a way of life would cease to exist in a very short period of time unless drastic steps were taken to utilize innate tribal energies and abilities to meet the challenges of mere survival. While it is recognized that today's Indian tribes have made cultural adaptations to meet the social crisis that confronts them in our technological society, the adaptations have been symbolic rather than practical, as the recurring cycle of poverty and human despair readily and visibly attests. In short, there exists no flexible and comprehensive approach to solving the social problems induced by the introduction of the reservation system in the last century, and by its perpetuation in this century as the only method for the enhancement of active American Indian participation in the mainstream of American society.

Ironically enough, it is commonly assumed that the reservation system provides the necessary social and educational institutions for enhancing tribal social mobility, and thus it is maintained that the reservation system will lead to successful Indian participation in the greater American society. However, if the Indians do not have ultimate control over their own destinies and remain entrapped within the narrow confines of reservation administration and government, they cannot be expected to participate to any significant degree in the community affairs of modern America.

If the reservation system has created a pseudoculture in contrast to previous aboriginal cultures, a lack of knowledge of either way of life must be assumed, since research to date has not provided an impeccable insight into the universals that constitute the aboriginal Indian gestalt. Aboriginal and American Indian cultures contain certain universals, which are found in all societies of man and serve as primary needs and functions:

1. Language—the most important of all.
2. Status of the individual in the group. Who outranks whom?
3. Family and other social groups.
4. Methods for dealing with food, shelter, clothing, and other vital materials.
5. Government and law. These can be very informal but are always there.
6. Religion and ethics.
7. Systems for explaining natural phenomena—magic, mythology, and, lately, science.
8. Rules regarding property. Who owns what? Methods for barter and trade.
9. Art forms—the dance, stories, songs, poems, architecture, handicrafts, and design.[19]

Little is known of the total structural set of values devised by the aboriginal peoples to fit their tribal way of life, and even less is known of the actual functional aspects of the habits, customs, and traditions that provided the basis for compatible tribal living before the onset of Euro-American social and technological influence. While vestiges of the aboriginal cultures still exist on many reservations in America, a new and different practice of "Indianness" now prevails, and it is proving to be a cultural enigma that will go unresolved for many years to come.

The interest in today's American Indians was generated by the era of social unrest that marked the decade of the 1960s in America. Inclusive of this social movement was the plight of reservation people and the vast differences between the values of American Indians and of Americans in general. The uniqueness of the American Indian culture was predicated on a questionable set of values that were diametrically opposed to those of the average American citizen. No scientific attempt was made to differentiate between the known pre-reservation value systems and the accepted value system adhered to on today's reservations. The cultural traits observed among the present generation of Indians are somehow supposed to be representative of ancient tribal cultural characteristics, which for one reason or another have yet to be fully explained.

To further complicate the oversimplification of Indian cultural characteristics, the Indian people are categorized, according to observed stages of acculturation and assimilation, as traditionalists, moderates, and progressives. Such an ordering of individual characteristics for the purpose of study and social clarification, or differentiation, and as a means for portraying the dynamics of contemporary Indian cultures, is inferred to be an academic necessity in understanding the socioeconomic problems of Indian tribes. The total lack of real knowledge of the personal views or philosophies of the Indians so glibly classified as traditionalists, moderates, and progressives must be taken into consideration when attempting to understand the academic generalizations that form the basis for the study of the contemporary American Indian. The lack of knowledge of the past and present American Indian gestalt is conceded by most authors of materials pertaining to the Indians, but this academic actuality is understated in nonspecific terminology.

At the same time, the general descriptions of reservation cultures and individual characteristics follow a questionable pattern of academic procedure. For instance, conservative or traditionalist Indians can never be fully appreciated (as they should be if respect for the individual is truly an authentic American value) so long as academic authors continue to display the questionable ambiguity and ignorance of the traditionalist philosophy that we find in the following assertion.

The Conservatives still adhere to their own religion and the old cultural pattern. They believe that the problems their tribe has today are the results of the abandonment of the old way of life. The Gods are not happy because the Indian people have turned from their former beliefs toward the white man's way.[20]

In reality, academia knows neither the religion nor the cultural patterns of Indian traditionalists, and without such knowledge there is no basis for passing judgment on the topical beliefs and customs of the Indian people. Furthermore, academia must be able to provide a logical rationale that would justify the implication that an individual's religion or cultural pattern is without merit simply because it has no analogy in the American system of cultural values. Perhaps, in fact, the traditionalists or conservatives are worthy of emulation, for, though living in a culture contrived by congressional legislation and medieval religiosity, they subtly refuse to live as a contrived society lives, or to be governed by a contrived set of values. The failure to distinguish between strengths and weaknesses in tribal values lies at the social, political, and economic crux of Indian problems in American society.

Some Progress Made in Understanding the Problem

Of important educational consequence is the current trend of teaching for ethnic literacy,[21] which compares and contrasts certain distinct cultural differences as they relate to one another in the total social scheme of American ethnicity. Educational materials pertaining to American Indians note, in particular, the vast cultural differences between Indians and non-Indians, which seem to be unsurmountable obstacles to any full understanding and appreciation of the contrasting cultures. Cultural differences between the dominant non-Indian society and the Indian society tend to reflect a need for educational oversimplification of the problems studied in order to justify the national social status quo in terms of implied avenues of social mobility.[22] In the teaching of ethnic diversity, the non-Indian way of life is portrayed as having values more conducive to success in a highly technological and industrialized society—that is, future-orientation, time consciousness, saving, emphasis on youth, competition, and conquest of nature.[23] The Indian way of life, on the other hand, encompasses the values of present-orientation, lack of time consciousness, giving, respect for age, cooperation, and harmony with nature.[24]

Such generalizations, even when acknowledged as generalizations and therefore subject to exceptions,[25] are oversimplifications both in description and in conveying a preconceived representation of the way Indians and non-Indians may or may not be. If today's American Indians are present-oriented, for instance, there must be an intellectual attempt to determine why this trait has come to form an observable value in the modern Indian way of life. The concept of time utilized by aboriginal Americans in a more cultural environment cannot be functionally equated with the present time concepts of reservation people, whose life-style has been predetermined, for the most part, by non-Indian people. In essence, too little is known about what aboriginal "Indianness" was, what constitutes "Indianness" today, and what "Indianness" is to be in the future.

The generalizations about American Indians and their culture will continue to be a source of research and study for generations to come. A true knowledge of the composition of the Indian gestalt can only be acquired by deliberate and objective study of every facet of past and present Indian cultures and the value systems that contributed to a compatible way of tribal life. Only by a study of the integral components of the universals of the societies of man can an overall picture of the aboriginal way of life be reconstructed, and this will clarify the innate qualities of the Indian customs and values that were so vital in the social, political, and economic aspects of tribal existence.

At present, due to the lack of sufficient knowledge about the Indian societal structure and the dynamics of tribal living, only minimal efforts are being made to bring about an objective understanding of the American Indian way of life. A qualitative and systematic study of the longitudinal heritage of today's Indians must be continued if a more valid explanation of Indian values is to be achieved. Moreover, it is imperative that the American public at large become familiar with the Indian and his culture if the Indian way of life is someday to become an innate and integral component of the American way of life. Educators must assume the responsibility for initiating and facilitating this transition by developing and implementing functional approaches for social change.

NOTES

1. D'Arcy McNickle, *The Indian Tribes of the United States: Ethnic and Cultural Survival* (London: Oxford Press, 1968), p. 10.

2. Wilcomb E. Washburn, *Red Man's Land—White Man's Law: A Study of the Past and Present Status of the American Indian* (New York: Charles Scribner's Sons, 1971), p. 22.

3. Peter I. Rose, *They and We: Racial and Ethnic Relations in the United States* (New York: Random House, 1964), p. 51.

4. Eleazar Wheelock, "Of the Original Design, Rise, Progress and Present State of the Indian Charity-School in Lebanon, Connecticut," in *Social History of American Civilization*, vol. 1: *Colonial Times to 1860*, ed. Rena L. Vassar (Chicago: Rand McNally, 1965), p. 54.

5. Bernard W. Sheehan, *Seeds of Extinction: Jeffersonian Philanthropy and the American Indian* (Chapel Hill, University of North Carolina Press, 1973), p. 4.

6. Ibid., p. 11.

7. *Indian Education: Historical Status of Indian Education* (Washington: Department of the Interior, Bureau of Indian Affairs, Branch of Education, 1965), vol. 29, no. 423, p. 4.

8. Ibid.

9. Ibid.

10. Ibid.

11. Ibid.

12. Ibid., p. 5.

13 Virginia Armstrong Irving, *I Have Spoken: American History through the Voices of the Indians* (New York: Pocket Books, 1972), p. 100.

14. Clark Wissler, *Red Man Reservations* (New York: Collier Books, 1971), pp. 149-50.

15. Kirke Kickingbird and Karen Ducheneaux, *One Hundred Million Acres* (New York: Macmillan, 1973), p. xxvi.

16. Theodore W. Taylor, *The States and Their Indian Citizens* (Washington: Government Printing Office, 1972), p. 146.

17. Ibid.

18. Stuart Chase, *The Proper Study of Mankind: An Inquiry into the Science of Human Relations* (New York: Harper & Row, 1967), p. 79.

19. Ibid., p. 80.

20. Robert A. Roessel, Jr., "The Indian Child and His Culture," in *Teaching Multi-Cultural Populations: Five Heritages*, ed. Donald P. DeNevi and James C. Stone (New York: Van Nostrand Reinhold, 1971), p. 306.

21. James A. Banks, "Teaching for Ethnic Literacy: A Comparative Approach," *Social Education* 37, no. 8 (December 1973): 738.

22. Roessel, "The Indian Child and His Culture," p. 306.

23. Ibid., p. 307.

24. Ibid.

25. Ibid., p. 306.

BIBLIOGRAPHY

BANKS, JAMES. "Teaching for Ethnic Literacy: A Comparative Approach." *Social Education* 37, no. 8 (December 1973).

BROPHY, WILLIAM A., and ABERLE, SOPHIE D. *The Indian: America's Unfinished Business*. Norman: University of Oklahoma Press, 1966.

CHASE, STUART. *The Proper Study of Mankind: An Inquiry into the Science of Human Relations*. New York: Harper & Row, 1967.

ELSON, RUTH MILLER. *Guardians of Tradition: American Schoolbooks of the Nineteenth Century*. Lincoln, University of Nebraska Press, 1964.

GROSSACK, MARTIN, and GARDNER, HOWARD. *Man and Men: Social Psychology as Social Science*. Scranton: International Textbook Co., 1970.

JACKSON, HELEN HUNT. *A Century of Dishonor: The Early Crusade for Indian Reform*. New York: Harper & Row, 1965.

KICKINGBIRD, KIRKE, and DUCHENEAUX, KAREN. *One Hundred Million Acres*. New York: Macmillan, 1973.

ROESSEL, ROBERT A., JR. "The Indian Child and His Culture." In *Teaching Multi-Cultural Populations: Five Heritages*. Edited by DONALD P. DENEVI and JAMES C. STONE. New York: Van Nostrand Reinhold, 1971.

TAYLOR, THEODORE W. *The States and Their Indian Citizens*. Washington: Government Printing Office, 1972.

U.S. Department of the Interior. *The United States Indian Service: A Sketch of the Development of the Bureau of Indian Affairs and of Indian Policy*. Washington: Bureau of Indian Affairs, 1962.

WASHBURN, WILCOMB E. *Red Man's Land—White Man's Law: A Study of the Past and Present Status of the American Indian*. New York: Charles Scribner's Sons, 1971.

WISE, JENNINGS C. *The Red Man in the New World Drama: A Politico-Legal Study with a Pageantry of American Indian History*. New York: Macmillan, 1971.

WISSLER, CLARK. *Red Man Reservations*. New York: Collier Books, 1971.

YOUNG, ROBERT. *Historical Backgrounds for Modern Indian Law and Order*. Albuquerque: Bureau of Indian Affairs, Division of Law and Order, 1969.

Summary

by

Walter K. Beggs

Dean Emeritus, Teachers College
University of Nebraska

Each of the preceding essays has outlined in some detail the paramount educational needs of one of the nation's significant and crucially important minority groups. Obviously there are other, and equally significant, populations within our society which might have been included. While the inclusion of these would have added some interest and perhaps a better understanding of the complexities of this great national dilemma, the predetermined length of the book precluded this possibility.

As noted in the Introduction, none of the authors was instructed or delimited in his approach or the manner in which he would present his material. As a result, and as would be expected under these circumstances, considerable difference is evidenced in each presentation. Robbins and James, writing respectively of Native American Indians and black Americans, approach the subject from a historical perspective. Castañeda relies on his bibliographic sources to acquaint the reader with the history of the Mexican-American population, and devotes his essay largely to the immediate and pressing problems of the group. In a previous interview with this author, he noted that the ancestors of some Mexican-Americans were on the soil of what is now part of the United States long before Columbus made his voyage, while others arrived as late as the day before yesterday.

In so stating Castañeda pinpoints one of the salient considerations of the minority issue. As we shall note presently, the current problems of what some analysts call the great disenfranchised minorities can be generalized. But each has its own peculiar root system in the culture, and the circumstances of the evolution of its relationship with the dominant strain in American society varied considerably in the dimensions of time and space and intensity.

James devotes a great deal of time to exploring the nature and the meaning, to say nothing of the injustices, of the period of bondage through which the black citizens of this country passed on their tortuous way first to freedom, then to citizenship, and finally to the great reach for equality, which has not yet been achieved even though significant gains have been made. The educational problems of black Americans cannot be understood, and, parenthetically, no permanent solutions will be found, until it is realized that educational problems are offshoots of greater national problems. And the national problems

—poverty, crowding in the cities, effective use of the nation's man-power, welfare, health, and many others—are not confined to one segment of the population. Hence race, although a significant element, is not the only consideration in the attempt to solve the issues in the black community.

James also makes another point, which is equally true of the Indian and the Mexican-American communities. The black community, he notes, is a diverse group. Many of its members hold the same values, have the same aspirations, and approach life in the same way as their counterparts in the general national population.

This very diversity makes the solution to the educational problems of the black community more complex. Most blacks find the process of securing the tools necessary for upward mobility more difficult because of their "blackness," and for the same reason many more of them are concentrated at the lower levels of the socioeconomic scale. And while James does not make the point specifically, it is implicit in what he concludes—there is still considerable prejudice and bigotry in the white community, which makes the solution to the problems much more difficult, and may well be a major element in the very existence of the problems.

James gives no formula for the solution of these enigmas; he offers no panaceas. He does insist that minority educators be granted full partnership in determining what needs to be done, and how. He does not appear to want, or to think desirable, a separate black community. The solution, as he sees it, is a frontal attack on the nation's social and economic problems and its cultural dislocations, using all the resources available; certainly among the best resources are the ability and the thinking of the minority groups themselves, which must be given a full share in the operation. And finally, while the schools cannot solve the problems, they must play a central role in developing a society in which *all* citizens of the nation have free access to the principles of freedom and democracy.

Robbins, in his analysis of the present Native American Indian situation, takes a somewhat different approach. While his treatment is historical, he generally ignores what most critics of the handling of Indian affairs consider the gross mistreatment of the tribes, if not the criminal theft of their property and the deliberate abrogation of their rights. He makes only passing reference to the original encroachment of the uninvited foreign explorers on the Indian preserves. He mentions but makes no special issue of the gradual shouldering aside of the native population by the growing nation, and he gives scant attention to the sorry spectacle of the sovereign government of the United States making treaty after treaty with the tribes—in order to give some sort of legal sanction to forcibly acquiring the land—and then callously breaking practically every one of them.

But in another way his indictment of the dominant culture, which he calls the Euro-American system, for its treatment of the Indians is the most severe and damning we have encountered. Robbins's concern is with a more subtle injury. In the process of attempting to "Christianize," to "civilize," and later to "democratize" the aboriginal tribes who originally possessed the continent—a civilization was destroyed! It was a culture with unique languages, family and social structures, methods for providing the necessities of life, government, law, religion—mores and customs. It was a tribal society, with differences from tribe to tribe, but also with many common elements. And it was a satisfactory and fulfilling and probably a beautiful system to the people who lived in and enjoyed it.

The American government, the missionaries, and perhaps a few of the frontier settlers made some effort to provide a few crude institutions and the educational avenues to help the Indians adopt the new way of life. It should be noted that in these efforts no options were proposed—it was adopt the new way of life—or else. Some of the Indians obviously made the transition—willingly or not—and their progeny have merged with the dominant strain. Many died in the abortive military efforts to protect their preserve and the old way of life. In relation to the size of the nation now, only a pitifully small handful of Indians are left as the legacy of one of the most inept, unhappy, and ugly chapters of American history.

There are perhaps a half-million Indians—probably a liberal estimate. What about their educational needs?

Robbins points out that their situation is an ambiguous, unhappy state of affairs. They live in a social and political and economic impasse, contrived for them by a government which has, of necessity, been forced into a position of unwilling benevolence; the Indians, in turn, have contrived ways to resist adopting an unwanted value structure and way of life while appearing to live in it—at least at its periphery on the reservations. But in the process the people themselves have been terribly degraded—and the real essence of the once proud and beautiful Indian culture has been eroded—perhaps beyond recovery.

But Robbins wants an attempt made to recover it. Like James, he has no specific formula to offer, and no explicit ways of doing this. If we interpret him correctly, he suggests that every attempt be made to recapture the major elements of the original aboriginal cultures.

Let both the modern Indians and American society generally study and attempt to understand the beauty and meaning of these societies. Then develop a workable frame of reference, through which the Indian population can, if it chooses, live by the old mores and customs — or meld these with the values of modern American society — or reject them in favor of the prevailing social scheme of things. It's a big order, a great challenge, perhaps an "impossible dream" — but an educational opportunity worthy of American society's best efforts.

Castañeda, in his treatment of the educational needs of Mexican-Americans, critically examines some of the assumptions which have pervaded educational thinking in the United States for many years — in fact, throughout our history. In the first place, like Robbins and James, and much more explicitly, he rejects the melting-pot thesis as a viable objective for the American school system. In a nation made up of many different backgrounds and ethnic compositions, it is absurd to present a predetermined set of values and cultural accouterments to all learners, regardless of their abilities and backgrounds, or their needs and desires. Not only is it absurd, it is especially damaging when the explicit intent of such a process is to enforce acceptance of, and conformity to, the so-called established system.

Castañeda identifies three major features of American democracy, and he notes that the schools have seriously jeopardized one of these. Because it is the opinion of the editors that he has isolated the nub of the minority education problem in this concept, we are going to quote his statement:

While American public education has continually attempted to keep alive the principles of political and economic democracy, it has been antagonistic to the principle of *cultural democracy*, the right of every American child to remain identified with his own ethnic, racial, or social group while at the same time exploring mainstream cultural forms with regard to language, heritage, values, cognition, and motivation.

This position goes considerably beyond, and substantially broadens, the concept of the American dream as Adams envisioned it, because it not only grants the right of every person to attain his fullest stature, but it also grants him the right to select, or at the very least to examine, some options concerning the type of social and cultural frame of reference through which he will attain that stature. This approach also sharply challenges some assumptions on which the public education system has based its orientation to the minority groups. The assumptions, implicit in such concepts as "culturally deprived," "underprivileged," "disadvantaged," and so on, have been the basic rationale of the system for compensatory education and other ameliorative efforts to meet the needs of its minority children.

Castañeda proposes that educators recognize, once and for all, that we are dealing with cultural pluralism. Rather than assume that some children are culturally deprived or disadvantaged — they should be recognized for what they are, culturally different, and the educational system should adjust accordingly. In a multicultural society, the schools must face the inescapable fact that children arrive at school not only in many stages of development, but from many different and widely varying backgrounds.

So we must develop programs of multicultural education. But these must cut across all the strata of the nation's educational system. Ethnic studies programs relevant to many minority groups have appeared on a number of campuses, but, while this is a start, it is not nearly enough. The universities and colleges, particularly in their teacher education divisions, must devote much research, time, and resources to developing programs to produce a generation of teachers much better prepared to deal with the exigencies of a multicultural situation in the schools. At the very least, teachers should approach their first assignments knowing that they will find children with particular ethnic backgrounds and unique linguistic heritages, and, in some instances, that they will meet learners so isolated from the mainstream thrust of the schools that they find themselves in an alien world.

The schools must be flexible enough not only to recognize the wide differences in learners and their backgrounds, but to develop a learning environment broad enough to avoid isolating any child. The curricular offerings, the teaching strategies, the climate of acceptance — all of these factors must be integrated in such a way that they do not violate a child's sense of identity with his ethnic group, and at the same time help him to develop a sense of identity with the mainstream society.

But, how to do it? What changes will be required in the school system by way of structure and organization and curricular offerings? What adjustments will need to be made in teacher attitudes and teaching styles, and strategies of approach to the special needs of different types of learners? More importantly, where does the beginning of reform cut into the cycle? Is it at the pretraining level; the in-service patterns of retraining; the point of selection of teacher-training candidates; the policies of reemployment of teachers, eliminating those who do not measure up – or perhaps at all of these levels and points on a broad frontal attack?

Of one thing we can be sure. These problems and issues highlight the trauma of a nation trying to develop a social philosophy consistent with its cherished dream of a multiethnic, culturally pluralistic society, and because of this they will plague the educational system for many years to come.

It has to be a philosophy, now, which will encompass the desires, the ambitions, the needs, the rights – and often the seemingly paranoid and unreasonable demands – of many and varied minority populations.